Emergency Department

Triage
Handbook

Aspen Series in Emergency and Trauma Nursing

Gail Pisarcik Lenehan, RN, MS, CS, Series Editor

Psychiatric Clinical Nurse Specialist
Emergency Department
Massachusetts General Hospital
Boston, Massachusetts

**Clinical Guidelines for Emergency Care Nursing:
Standardized Nursing Care Plans**
Susan Moore
Deborah A. Charlson

Pediatric Trauma Nursing
Connie Joy

Managing Emergency Nursing Services
Iris C. Frank

Quick Reference to Pediatric Emergency Nursing
Donna Ojanen Thomas

Emergency Department

Triage
Handbook

Lisa Molitor, ARNP, MSN, CEN, CCRN
Nurse Practitioner
Alachua County Organization
for Rural Needs
Brooker Township, Florida
Shands Hospital
University of Florida
Gainesville, Florida

Aspen Series in Emergency and Trauma Nursing
Gail Pisarcik Lenehan, Series Editor

AN ASPEN PUBLICATION®
Aspen Publishers, Inc.
Gaithersburg, Maryland
1992

Library of Congress Cataloging-in-Publication Data

Molitor, Lisa.
Emergency department triage handbook/ by Lisa Molitor.
p. cm. — (Aspen series in emergency and trauma nursing)
Includes bibliographical references.
Includes index.
ISBN 0-8342-0283-2
1. Triage (Medicine)—Handbooks, manuals, etc. 2. Emergency
nursing—Handbooks, manuals, etc. I. Title. II Series. [DNLM:
1. Emergencies—nursing—handbooks. 2. Emergency Service,
Hospital—organization & administration—handbooks.
3. Triage—handbooks. WY 39 M725e]
RT120.E4M65 1992
616.02'5—dc20
DNLM/DLC
for Library of Congress 91-31517
CIP

Aspen Publishers, Inc., grants permission for photocopying for limited
personal or internal use. This consent does not extend to other kinds of
copying, such as copying for general distribution, for advertising or pro-
motional purposes, for creating new collective works, or for resale. For
information, address Aspen Publishers, Inc., Permissions Department,
200 Orchard Ridge Drive, Suite 200, Gaithersburg, Maryland 20878.

The authors have made every effort to ensure the accuracy of the
information herein, particularly with regard to drug selection
and dose. However, appropriate information sources should be
consulted, especially for new or unfamiliar drugs or procedures.
It is the responsibility of every practitioner to evaluate the appro-
priateness of a particular opinion in the context of actual clinical
situations and with due consideration to new developments. Authors, editors, and the publisher cannot be held responsible for
any typographical or other errors found in this book.

Editorial Services:
Barbara Priest

Library of Congress Catalog Card Number: 91-31517
ISBN: 0-8342-0283-2

Printed in the United States of America

1 2 3 4 5

Table of Contents

Contributors

Mary D. Beasley, RN, BSN

Nursing Supervisor
Surgical Intensive Care Unit
Shands Hospital
Gainesville, Florida

Paula Turvy McCarty, RN

Clinical Nurse Specialist
Emergency Department
Gainesville VA Medical Center
Gainesville, Florida

Susan W. Somerson, RN, MSN, CEN

Clinical Nurse Specialist
Emergency Department
Presbyterian Medical Center of Philadelphia
Philadelphia, Pennsylvania

Donna Ojanen Thomas, RN, MSN, CEN

Director
Emergency Department
Primary Children's Medical Center
Salt Lake City, Utah

Ramona J. Trebilcock, PhD, RN

Director
Medical/Surgical/Behavioral Services
UCSD Medical Center
San Diego, California

Preface

In the triage area, and throughout the emergency department (ED), the caregiver's primary concerns are "How sick is this patient? Can he or she wait for definitive care, or should the patient be seen immediately?" The needs of life-threatened patients are usually obvious, but it is the patient with more subtle presentations who provides practitioners with the greatest challenges and the most professional anxiety. This book was designed to help ED practitioners cover all the bases in assessing patients. A variety of the most commonly encountered patient presentations have been reviewed and analyzed using the traditional subjective/objective/assessment/plan format to facilitate systematic evaluation and documentation. Several sections also include a "Think" subsection, designed to help alert practitioners to potentially serious causes of the signs and symptoms identified. Pediatric emergency triage requires special diligence; to this end there is a separate section addressing pediatric triage needs. Finally, the appendices include brief, practical tips on how to elicit various parts of the history and physical assessment.

The reader will note that many sections of this book take the practitioner beyond the usual scope of triage assessment and provide information that may be more detailed than one would expect to use in the triage setting. It is the authors' hope that ED practitioners will use this book to assess their patients throughout the ED arena, and we have provided information that will be helpful in that endeavor.

ABOUT THIS MANUAL

This manual has been written and edited by a group of ED nurses with substantial experience in emergency care, triage, and assessment of patients. Its contents are the product of many combined years of experience, training, and observation. It is designed to help practitioners organize their thinking while they are conducting assessment and triage in the emergency setting.

This manual has been designed to supplement the existing skills of ED practitioners. In many cases, standard professional judgment will dictate the interventions that are applied; and in other cases, department or institutional protocol will dictate the actions taken by health care professionals. For these reasons, in most sections the plans recommended by the authors reiterate basic interventions rather than dictate particular interventions. In all sections, where certain critical actions are required, we have tried to provide standard information. The user's discretion will always determine what actions are taken in caring for a patient.

To use this manual to its fullest extent, the reader should refer to the index for cross-referencing of the various presenting complaints covered. The reader should also refer to the appendices for more detailed evaluation tips and techniques. The appendices include helpful information about physical assessment and making use of blood gas information, a quick reference of cardiac dysrhythmias, and a number of other topics.

It is the hope of the authors and editors of this book that it will help ED practitioners do their important jobs a little better and with a little more confidence.

Acknowledgments

This book was made possible by the group of very fine emergency department practitioners who wrote and edited various sections. I owe them my deep respect and gratitude.

I am also grateful to Dr Sandra Seymour for her early editorial assistance, her long-time support, and the excellent standards she has consistently set for me.

Finally, I owe my greatest debt of professional gratitude to Ms Leah Feldman and Dr Peter Gearen, who have been role models to me for many years and whose uncompromising patient care continues to inspire me.

Introduction

TRIAGE AND ASSESSMENT: THE BASICS

If the nursing process comprises assessment, analysis, problem identification, intervention, and evaluation, then nowhere else is this process more alive than in the emergency department (ED). Each component of this process is vital to the well being, indeed the very lives, of our patients. Perhaps in no other arena of the hospital setting are a nurse's skills more valuable than in the ED triage area. The practice of effective triage requires a combination of talents: organized thinking sprinkled with a healthy dose of intuition; well-developed, time-efficient history-taking skills; accurate and concise written documentation; and sharp physical assessment skills. The nurse fills the important role of public relationist for the department and the institution. He or she must have a constant awareness of the legal environment. On occasion, the triage nurse assumes the role of health educator. He or she is also the patient's confidant and advocate. On top of this, in high-stress situations, the triage nurse must accurately assess, set priorities, and intervene in the shortest possible time. She or he must also be highly adaptable and able to accommodate the needs of an ever-changing patient population without notice. There is no question that the role of triage nurse is one of the most demanding in nursing today.

The history of the triageur is both interesting and noble. Triage, which is a French verb, translates as "to sort" in English. The original role of the triageur was to evaluate battlefield casualties, discriminating the salvageable patient from the mortally injured or dead. In this way, it was assured that limited resuscitation resources were not spent on those for whom there was no hope. In peacetime, the work of the triage nurse takes on a different complexion. In the typical ED, the triage nurse acts a gatekeeper, sorting emergently ill, urgently ill, walking wounded, and healthy patients into manageable groups, thus ensuring the best use of the ED's resources while simultaneously ensuring expedient care for those who need it most.

Documentation with the SOAP Format

As is the case with all facets of nursing, documentation is a primary responsibility in the triage area. The triage nurse's note serves to describe the patient on arrival in the ED via the subjective and objective data collected, documents the nursing assessment of the patient, and documents the plan of care for that patient in the period immediately following arrival.

The SOAP format has been widely adopted as the preferred method of documentation. SOAP is the acronym for *s*ubjective/*o*bjective/*a*ssessment/*p*lan. This format reflects the nursing process and serves as an organizational framework for the triage process. Some nursing diagnosticians are now advocating the use of the SOAPIE format, which incorporates the *i*ntervention and *e*valuation components of the process. In many cases of triage nursing, the process will be completed by another practitioner who assumes care of the patient from the triage nurse. Our limiting of the acronym to *SOAP* in this text is not intended to discourage those other important phases of the nursing process. It simply is a fact of life in the ED that intervention and evaluation are rarely responsibilities of the triageur.

In collecting subjective data, the practitioner should limit himself or herself to the information that is provided verbally by the patient or another person providing the history. As a rule of thumb, subjective information should be limited to that which could be gathered over the telephone (ie; the patient's description of his or her signs/symptoms). Information gathered should include the patient's statement, in his or her own words, about the primary complaint. Quoted statements should be written with quotation marks. If the person providing the history is not the patient, that person and the relationship to the patient should be clearly identified.

Certain baseline information should always be elicited:

- *Allergies*: Documentation of allergies to medications is essential, but inquiry into food and environmental allergies can be helpful. Furthermore, the effect of the allergy should be described. For example, does the reported allergen nauseate the patient or produce respiratory distress?

- *Immunization status*: This information is important in the assessment of all children, even if the reported symptoms do not relate to the immune status. The ED sometimes serves as the entry point of children into the health care system, and referral for immunizations or other basic health care can be facilitated by ED personnel. Tetanus toxoid (or booster) status should be determined if the patient's sequelae involve a break in the skin. Ask the date of the most recent booster, not simply whether the patient is up to date.

- *Menstrual history*: The date of last menstrual period should be elicited in all women of child-bearing age. This is an obvious point in women with obstetric/gynecologic complaints but should be documented in all women, given the likelihood that they will require X-ray examination and/or medications. Likewise, the woman who describes herself as postmenopausal should be questioned carefully.

- *Medications*: The patient should be asked to be as specific as possible about medications, including over-the-counter medications, home remedies, vitamins, and oral contraceptives. Include information about dosage, frequency, and total duration of time on medications. Such information can be helpful in determining the source of various problems.

• *Self-care attempted*: Document any self-care measures that may have been taken, along with any response the measures may have produced.

Objective information is that which can be elicited by the nurse without verbal input from the patient. Signs that can be seen, palpated, auscultated, or smelled fall into this category. As a general rule, one should elicit subjective information before collecting objective data. Physical findings should then be validated with reiteration of the patient's description of symptoms. Objective data should include negative as well as positive findings. Such notations help demonstrate thorough evaluation on the part of the nurse.

Once the data collection is complete, the assessment is formulated. It is important that the triage nurse limit himself or herself to nursing assessment and/or nursing diagnosis in the triage situation. The primary reason for this, apart from issues of professional practice, is the legal risk of making the equivalent of a medical diagnosis on the basis of the limited information elicited in the triage area. Furthermore, should the nurse's assessment, stated medically, conflict with the final medical diagnosis for the patient, the conflicting assessments on the part of the nurse and physician could be difficult to defend in a court of law. The assessment statement should include, in addition to the actual assessment phrase and/or nursing diagnosis, a phrase documenting the nurse's assessment of the relative severity of the patient's illness.

The plan formulated for the patient on the basis of the nursing assessment is the fourth component of the SOAP process. The plan should be as specific as possible and clearly reflect the relative urgency of the situation. It should also include any interventions carried out by the triage nurses. The practitioner who will assume responsibility for the patient's care should be identified in the note, along with the time at which the responsibility is assumed. Should the situation call for some delay in the progress of the patient's visit, as is the case in some busy EDs when the patient's condition is nonurgent, that should be documented as well.

FEAR OF THE UNKNOWN

Everyone working in the health care industry today has a heightened awareness of the potential for exposure to communicable diseases. In the ED, the patient population represents every facet of our society. The history of many ED patients is frequently unknown or unclear, and occasionally the history may be purposefully misrepresented. In this setting, the policy that makes the most sense for any practitioner is this: Practice defensively. Gloves should be worn when handling any body fluid, and isolation should be instituted in the triage area if there is an indication of active communicable disease.

Concerns about liability are a fact of life in these times. The practice of emergency care involves a component of liability risk that is unique to the ED setting: The patients are largely unknown to their caretakers, and the relationship between patient and caregiver is often quite brief. These features imply two basic approaches to caring for patients in the ED: (1) Err conservatively, and (2) document, document, document. A suspicious approach in the triage area includes careful history taking and careful requestioning after the physical examination has been completed.

THE VITAL SIGNS

The admission vital signs should be taken and documented by the triage nurse. Although the vital signs are usually considered part of the objective data, careful evaluation of vital signs is so important that it deserves separate discussion.

Temperature

Core temperature is most closely related to rectal temperature. In any patient situation in which an absolutely accurate temperature is important, a rectal measurement should be taken. Children younger than 6 or 7 years of age are generally unreliable about keeping the thermometer under the tongue, and it is easy to get an inaccurate reading in this population from the oral route. There is also a real risk of children biting the thermometer. Furthermore, to allow for accurate comparison of temperature to the history, the nurse should evaluate a rectal temperature and a temperature taken at the site the child's caregiver has used.

Pulse

The radial pulse should be counted for at least 30 seconds to include several inspiratory and expiratory cycles. Any variation in rhythm, unless clearly related to a benign sinus dysrhythmia, should be assessed for at least 60 seconds and further evaluated on a cardiac monitor. Regularity as well as irregularity should be documented. Comparison of apical and radial pulses is helpful in patients whose history suggests that they may have a deficit. The carotid pulse remains the most reliable site of pulse assessment in adult patients who are hemodynamically unstable. The brachial pulse is the preferred site of assessment in children. Pedal pulses should be evaluated in patients with hemodynamic instability.

Respirations

Respiratory rate should be counted for at least 30 seconds in all patients and for 60 seconds in patients with any sort of respiratory distress. The pattern, depth, and ease of respirations should be documented.

Blood Pressure

Blood pressures should be taken on all patients, including young infants. All Korotkoff sounds should be documented. Measurement of blood pressure in both arms is indicated whenever a patient's presenting complaint suggests a possible discrepancy or when syncope is part of the history.

Orthostatic Vital Signs

Orthostatic vital signs should be measured whenever hemodynamic instability is suspected, if the patient's condition allows. An increase in pulse rate of 20 beats/min when supine measurements are compared to upright measurements is considered significant. A decrease in systolic blood pressure of 20 mm Hg is considered significant in the same positional comparison.

Patient Weight

All pediatric patients should be weighed, not only to help chart growth but to allow for expedient calculation of medication dosages. In cases where fluid resuscitation is required, a baseline weight is most helpful in calculating fluid therapy.

Part I

Adult Emergency Triage

Section 1

Cardiac

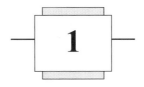

CHEST PAIN

Paula Turvy McCarty
Lisa Molitor, ed.

Subjective

- Location of pain (cardiac pain is typically midchest or substernal)
- Generalized or localized
- Radiating to arms, jaw, neck, subscapular area
- Duration and frequency of pain (time and mode of onset)
    1. Stable angina usually lasts 30 seconds to 30 minutes
    2. Unstable angina usually lasts more than 30 minutes
    3. MI usually lasts more than 45 minutes
- Quality or intensity of pain (quantitate on scale of 1 to 10): sharpness, dullness, cramping, crushing, squeezing, tightness, "someone sitting on my chest," fullness, indigestion, tearing, burning, mild chest discomfort
- Precipitating factors of pain: exercise, walking, intercourse, eating, resting, coughing, trauma, strain, anxiety, deep breathing
- Concomitant symptoms/angina equivalents*

1. Shortness of breath*, nausea*, vomiting, diaphoresis*, dizziness*, syncope*, anxiety, skin color change, palpitations
2. Painful cough (suggests pleural irritation)
3. Gastrointestinal symptoms
4. Relationship of pain to eating or not eating, particularly fried or fatty foods
5. History of hiatal hernia and/or symptoms of reflux

- Pain alleviated by

  1. Medications (angina usually relieved by nitroglycerine, Nitrobid paste, Isordil, inderal, rest, and/or oxygen)
  2. Rest
  3. Positioning
  4. Other treatment (reassurance, anxiety reduction, oxygen, etc)
  5. Eating or not eating
  6. Antacids

- Past medical history (previous MIs, history of surgery, allergies, emotional trauma, increased stress)

- History of trauma (penetrating injury, blunt trauma, strain from lifting or the like, severe coughing)

- Medications (for cardiac disease, blood pressure, chronic obstructive pulmonary disease; tranquilizers, antibiotics for respiratory infections, β blockers)

- Risk factors

  1. Family history, increased cholesterol, increased blood pressure, previous MI, age, gender, race, diabetes, cigarette smoking, obesity, stress, alcohol use
  2. Recreational drug use, particularly cocaine, crack, or intravenous drugs

Note: Patients with diabetes mellitus may not have classic chest pain secondary to chronic neuropathies and should be carefully questioned about the presence of atypical chest pain and/or angina equivalents.

Objective

- Vital signs
    1. Pulse (regular or irregular, weak or strong, fast or slow; pulse integrity, rate)
    2. Carotid pulses (thrill/bruit)
    3. Blood pressure (increased—catecholamine release; decreased—cardiogenic shock)
    4. Respirations (shortness of breath, tachypnea, depth, splinting or guarding, bilateral chest wall movement)
- General appearance
    1. Upright, relaxed carriage or doubled-over or uncomfortable posture
    2. Clutching, rubbing chest
    3. Level of anxiety
    4. Painful grimacing
    5. Ability to answer questions coherently
- Skin (touching patient to obtain vital signs will allow for assessment of skin temperature and moisture)
    1. Color (pale, pink, cyanotic)
    2. Capillary fill time (good estimate of efficiency of tissue perfusion)
    3. Presence of diaphoresis
    4. Temperature (central and peripheral)
- Extremities (pulse quality and equality in all four extremities)
- Neurologic
    1. Level of consciousness
    2. Anxiety, restlessness (Anxiety and restlessness are signs of pain and/or early hypoxia; lethargy may represent late hypoxia)
    3. Presence of lethargy
    4. Subjective "feeling of doom" (occurs in acute MI)
- Reproduction of pain (can pain be reproduced by palpation, deep breathing, change of position?)
- Abdomen
    1. Concomitant abdominal pain
    2. Soft or rigid

  3. Presence of aortic bruit
  4. Femoral pulses

Assessment

- Chest pain with/without signs/symptoms of:
  1. Cardiac etiology (MI or angina)
  2. Gastrointestinal upset, especially esophageal spasm
  3. Respiratory/pulmonary disease (acute or chronic)
  4. Simple pneumothorax/tension pneumothorax
  5. Aortic aneurysm
  6. Costachondritis/chest wall pain
  7. Pericarditis/myocarditis
  8. Pulmonary embolism
- Document pertinent objective signs
- Include history of trauma if applicable

Plan

- Admit to examination room, stat physician evaluation if life-threatening condition is suspected
- In emergency or urgent situation, anticipate some or all of the following physician orders:
  1. Cardiac monitoring
  2. 12-Lead ECG
  3. Intravenous access
  4. Oxygen
  5. Chest x-ray examination
  6. Labs: CBC with differential, platelet count, renal profile, U/A, serum enzymes (CPK with bands, LDH, SGOT), PT, PTT, arterial blood gas measurement if streptokinase or t-PA are not anticipated, arterial lactic acid level; save extra tube of blood for type and cross-match
- Continuous bedside monitoring with physician and/or RN present if life-threatening condition is suspected

Think

1. *MI*: Index of suspicion increases with history of chest pain lasting longer than 30 to 45 minutes that is not relieved by nitrates, rest, and/or oxygen; past cardiac history; increased risk factors; abnormal cardiovascular findings; presence of angina equivalents; sense of "doom"

   - If ST elevation or Q waves are present in two or more leads, and/or are *not* present on previous ECGs, suspect MI
   - If pain radiates to left shoulder, arm, or jaw, suspect MI
   - If pain is reproduced by palpation, condition is unlikely to be MI
   - If pain radiates to back, abdomen, or legs, condition is unlikely to be MI, but may be associated with aneurysm or acute gastrointestinal event
   - If pain is stabbing, condition is unlikely to be MI

2. *Trauma*: Blunt trauma secondary to motor vehicle accident, fall, or blow to the chest may cause pulmonary and/or myocardial contusion or ruptured blood vessels in the thoracic cavity; penetrating trauma secondary to impaling object, gunshot wound, or knife wound may affect major blood vessels and cause hemothorax, pneumothorax

3. *Spontaneous, simple pneumothorax*: This may progress to tension pneumothorax; index of suspicion for pneumothorax increases with history of smoking, emphysema, chest trauma

4. *Pulmonary embolism*: Usually accompanied by obvious respiratory distress (see "Dyspnea"); index of suspicion increases with history of atrial fibrillation, use of oral contraceptives, decreased activity level, recent surgery, long bone fracture/surgery, late-term pregnancy, blood clots; pain is intense, localized, may increase with inspiration

FLUTTERING IN CHEST: HEART SKIPPING BEATS, PALPITATIONS

Lisa Molitor

See also "Dizziness/Syncope"

Subjective

- Onset of symptoms (duration, activity engaged in at time of onset)
- Concomitant weakness, dizziness, LOC
- Concomitant chest pain
- History of heart disease, angina, previous MI
- Associated with new medications, change in dosage of existing medications, ingestion of toxic substances (eg, cocaine, amphetamines)
- History of hypertension
- History of heart valve disorder

Objective

- Hemodynamic assessment
- Respiratory assessment
- Signs of congestive heart failure (jugular vein distension, cardiac gallop, rales, pedal edema, etc)
- Obtain rhythm strip and initiate continuous ECG monitoring per unit protocol, document rhythm

Assessment

- Subjective palpitations with/without evidence of dysrhythmia at presentation
- Subjective palpitations with evidence of ectopic beats (specify number per minute and type)

- Dysrhythmia with/without evidence of hemodynamic compromise

Plan

- ECG monitoring indicated; 12-Lead ECG as per protocol
- Stat physician evaluation if any of the following are present:
    1. Life-threatening dysrhythmias
    2. Chest pain
    3. Hemodynamic instability
    4. Signs of congestive heart failure
- Expedite physician evaluation otherwise

Think

1. Both ventricular and supraventricular tachycardias may produce a fluttering sensation with/without weakness and/or faintness
2. An irregular peripheral pulse cannot be assumed to be a benign sinus dysrhythmia unless variation in rhythm correlates perfectly with the respiratory cycle and unless more serious dysrhythmias are ruled out with electrophysiologic monitoring
3. Supraventricular tachycardias may involve a block at the site of the atrioventricular node. A patient with these sequelae may have a peripheral pulse rate in the normal range and still have a serious dysrhythmia; ECG monitoring must be instituted to ensure that this is not the case

Extremities

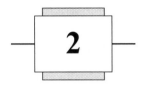

CALF PAIN

Lisa Molitor
Susan Somerson, ed.

See also "Extremity Pain"

Subjective

- Onset and duration of symptoms
- Location of pain—generalized or localized
- Character of pain
- Associated symptoms (swelling, fever, redness, shortness of breath)
- History of trauma
- History of clotting disorders
- History of immobilization
- History of unusual exertion
- History of smoking
- History of use of oral contraceptives
- History of recent surgery

Objective

- Appearance of involved leg, compared to contralateral leg
- Presence of limp
- Extremity examination
- Respiratory status
- Homan's sign
- Signs/symptoms of infection
- Integrity of skin

Assessment

- Calf pain with/without signs/symptoms suggestive of thrombus, thrombophlebitis, phlebitis
- Calf pain with history of trauma
- Calf pain with symptoms of compartment syndrome

Plan

- Stat physician evaluation if any of the following are present:
  1. Neurovascular symptoms
  2. Positive Homan's sign
  3. Associated respiratory distress/shortness of breath
  4. Associated fever and/or tachycardia
  5. Infection is suspected
  6. Compartment syndrome is suspected
- Expedite physician evaluation if:
  1. Pain is severe
  2. Obvious deformity is present (immobilize affected area)

Think

  1. Deep vein thrombosis

2. Compartment syndrome—may occur with direct trauma or overexertion
3. Occult fracture

FINGER PAIN

Lisa Molitor

Subjective

- Onset and duration of symptoms
- Associated numbness
- Evaluate skin integrity; particularly note circumferential skin tears or burns
- Associated color change
- Associated temperature change
- Associated with trauma (if so, describe mechanism of injury)
- History of Raynaud's phenomenon, peripheral vascular disease

Objective

- Skin integrity
- Capillary refill
- Range of motion (if possible)
- Skin temperature
- Color
- Avoid extensive examination if patient has severe pain, if there is obvious deformity, or if area appears infected

Assessment

- Finger pain (specify) with/without evidence of:

1. Digital nerve injury, especially if hooking trauma has occurred
2. Trauma
3. Infectious process

- Vascular and/or neurologic compromise
- Fracture/dislocation

Plan

- Stat physician evaluation if appendage is at risk or if there has been circumferential interruption in skin integrity
- Do not ice
- Immobilize if care will be delayed

Think

1. Loss of blood flow may put finger at risk
2. Circumferential skin loss puts blood supply to distal finger at risk

JOINT PAIN/JOINT STIFFNESS

Lisa Molitor

Subjective

- Onset and duration of symptoms
- Character of pain (sharp, dull, aching, stabbing, throbbing)
- Concomitant trauma (if so, describe mechanism of injury)
- In prone populations, personal or familial history of sickle cell dyscrasia
- History of bleeding disorders

- Concomitant fever
- History of arthritis (rheumatoid or degenerative)
- Accompanied by swelling
- Associated with change in skin color and/or rash
- History of insect bites, particularly tick bite
- History of surgery in the affected area, particularly joint replacement surgery
- History of gout
- Medications currently in use

Objective

- General degree of distress
- Appearance of joint:
    1. Presence of obvious deformity
    2. Skin intact or broken
    3. Bruising present
    4. Erythematous
    5. Swelling present
    6. Exudate from breaks in skin or tracts of infection
- Evaluate bones and joints both distal and proximal to affected joint
- Evaluate vascular/circulatory status distal to affected joint, especially in cases of traumatic injury or if dislocation is suspected
- Passive and active range of motion (exacerbation of pain, reproduction of pain, stability of joint)
- Patient febrile and/or has signs/symptoms of systemic infection
- Joint warm to touch

Assessment

- Joint pain (identify joint involved) with/without:
    1. Associated trauma
    2. Evidence of infection

Plan

- Immobilize as per unit protocol
- Expedite physician evaluation if evidence of neurovascular compromise

Think

1. Occult trauma/abuse in children and elders
2. If a traumatic injury is suspected, splint the affected part
3. A septic joint may seed infection into the bloodstream, producing septicemia (if patient appears in toxic condition, evaluate hemodynamic status)
4. Knee pain often implies hip pathology

LIMPING

The primary concern in assessing the limping patient in the triage area is to differentiate limping from ataxia; see "Ataxia" for further guidelines. If the patient is determined to be limping, refer to one or more of the following sections, as appropriate: "Extremity Pain," "Back Pain," "Evaluation of Extremities," "Joint Pain/Joint Stiffness," and "Numbness/Tingling."

SHOULDER PAIN

Lisa Molitor

Subjective

- Onset and duration of symptoms
- Character of pain
- Associated with trauma to shoulder
- Associated with trauma to abdomen

- History of abdominal pain
- History of mononucleosis, leukemia, or other diseases likely to produce splenic congestion
- Cardiac history and/or presence of angina equivalents
- Accompanied by respiratory symptoms, especially shortness of breath, pain on inspiration

Objective

- Range of motion
- Pulse quality (compare to contralateral pulses)
- Color of distal tissues
- Capillary refill time
- Neurosensory examination
- General level of distress
- Hemodynamic assessment if patient has been traumatized or if splenic involvement is suspected
- Respiratory assessment if patient has had trauma to chest or if respiratory symptoms are present

Assessment

- Shoulder pain with/without history of trauma
- Shoulder pain with/without evidence of neurovascular compromise
- Shoulder pain with/without evidence of respiratory sequelae
- Shoulder pain with/without evidence of cardiac origin
- Shoulder pain with/without history of trauma

Plan

- Stat physician evaluation if:
  1. Pain is severe
  2. Evidence of neurovascular compromise is present

3. Patient is hemodynamically unstable, especially if pain may be associated with myocardial ischemia or splenic sequelae
4. Pain is suggestive of pulmonary embolism or pneumothorax, with/without shortness of breath

Think

1. Myocardial pain will sometimes masquerade as shoulder pain
2. Left shoulder pain has been associated with splenic irritation or rupture
3. Right shoulder pain has been associated with gallbladder inflammation
4. Shoulder pain is also associated with diaphragmatic irritation

Section 3

Eye, Ear, Nose, Throat, Neck, and Head

EAR PAIN (WITH/WITHOUT DISCHARGE)

Lisa Molitor

Subjective

- Duration and onset of symptoms
- Concomitant trauma
- Possibility of foreign body
- Accompanied by hearing loss
- Accompanied by vertigo
- Accompanied by fever
- Accompanied by bleeding and/or discharge (describe discharge: consistency, color, estimated amount)
- History of untreated dental caries, infections, etc.

Objective

- General appearance (including ability to ambulate without apparent vertigo)
- Evidence of infection ("toxic" appearance, fever)

- Evidence of trauma (bleeding, swelling, deformity, break in skin of pinna and/or surrounding tissues)
- Gross hearing acuity
- If vertigo and/or head trauma are present, conduct neurologic assessment
- Presence of lymphadenopathy in anterior/posterior cervical chains, preauricular nodes, and/or submandibular nodes
- Examine mouth for signs of infection, abscess, etc.
- Optional otoscopic examination

Assessment

- Ear pain with
  1. Fever
  2. History of trauma
  3. Hearing loss
  4. Signs/symptoms of infection
- Subjective ear pain without objective findings

Plan

- Stat physician evaluation if neurologic sequelae present, patient has high fever
- Expedite physician evaluation if above not suspected

Think

1. Tympanic membrane rupture
2. Systemic infection related to otitis
3. Patient with vertigo should not be permitted to ambulate

HEARING LOSS

Susan Somerson
Lisa Molitor, ed.

Subjective

- Onset and duration of symptoms (symptoms unilateral or bilateral)
  1. Acute, associated with trauma
     —Blow to head
     —Exposure to loud noise, proximal to explosion
     —Foreign body inserted in ear
     —Insect in ear
  2. Acute, *not* associated with trauma
     —Recent URI
     —Recent inflammation of external ear
  3. Chronic
     —History of excessive cerumen
- Accompanied by pain (unilateral or bilateral)
- Accompanied by discharge
  1. Blood
  2. Pus
  3. Clear fluid
- Recent activities
  1. Swimming
  2. Fireworks or other explosives
  3. Exposure to airplanes, helicopters, other large engines
  4. Type of employment (heavy industry, working without ear plugs)
- Age of patient (in a child who is irritable, assess for tugging at ear; see "Pediatric")
- Associated symptoms
  1. Vertigo
  2. Nausea, vomiting
  3. Dizziness
- Past medical history, including medications

Objective

- Appearance of ear(s)
- Tenderness
- Examine external ear for inflammation, signs of trauma
- Concomitant fever
- Discharge from ear
  1. Pus
  2. Blood
  3. Clear fluid
  4. Halo test on blood or clear fluid
- Evidence of trauma to face or head, assess for
  1. Battle's sign
  2. Raccoon eyes
- Examination of ear canal *(do not perform if suspicious of basilar skull fracture with CSF leak; see "Think" below)*
  1. Tympanic membrane intact
  2. Presence of foreign body
  3. Moving insect
  4. Erythematous, bulging tympanic membrane
  5. Erythema and/or edema of canal
- May conduct Rinne's test if appropriate

Assessment

- Acute hearing loss secondary to trauma
- Acute hearing loss secondary to suspected infectious process
- Chronic hearing loss secondary to obliteration of canal
- Hearing loss of unknown cause

Plan

Arrange expedited physician evaluation.

Think

1. *Acute hearing loss with evidence of facial/head trauma:* Consider basilar skull fracture, especially if Battle's sign or raccoon eyes are present; do not examine ear canal; perform halo test on sterile cloth if drainage is present; apply sterile dressing to ear and arrange immediate physician evaluation; apply cervical spine immobilization and monitor neurologic status
2. *Acute hearing loss with report of insect in ear:* Examine ear canal and ascertain whether tympanic membrane is intact; if intact, and unit protocol allows, consider instilling 1 to 2 drops of mineral oil to suffocate insect, stop movement, and decrease potential for membrane perforation by insect; do not instill anything if there is evidence of membrane perforation or if status of membrane integrity is unknown
3. Acute hearing loss with associated vertigo: Consider Meniere's syndrome, labyrinthitis

EYE PAIN

Susan Somerson
Lisa Molitor, ed.

Subjective

- Onset and duration of symptoms
- Circumstances surrounding onset of pain (acute or gradual, what patient was doing at time of onset)
- Character of pain
- Pain location (in eyeball or around it)
- Quadrant of eye in which pain is located
- History of exposure to ultraviolet light within previous 12 hours
- Contact lens wearer
- If change in vision is present:
  1. Acute or gradual

    2. One eye or both

    3. Diplopia

    4. Describe vision loss (eg, blurring, shadow, etc)

- Pain exacerbated with movement of eye
- Accompanied by photophobia
- Prior medical history and/or medications
- Previous history of ophthalmologic condition
- Recent use of cold medications, decongestants
- History of trauma
- Working in shop or around projectiles without safety glasses
- Working with chemicals that may have splashed in eye, particularly acids or alkaline substances
- History of fever

Objective

- Gross evaluation of visual acuity (Snellen chart)
- Examine for conjunctival injection and/or periorbital erythema
- Presence of central or peripheral injection
- Compare pupil size and reactivity
- Check EOMs
- Observe for presence of hyphema
- Observe regularity of pupil margin
- Observe for presence of tearing
- Observe for discharge and/or adherence of eyelids
- Observe for periorbital edema
- Observe for subconjunctival hemorrhage
- If history of trauma:
    1. Gently palpate orbital rim for crepitus and tenderness
    2. Observe symmetry of gaze
    3. Examine for anesthesia/hypesthesia in infraorbital region

4. Conduct halo test for presence of CSF rhinorrhea

Note: Do not palpate globe or force eyelids apart if there is a history of trauma or penetration

Assessment

- Painful eye with history of:
    1. Trauma
    2. Ultraviolet light exposure
    3. Chemical exposure
- Painful eye with possible intraocular pathology
    1. Detached retina
    2. Globe penetration
- Painful eye with signs/symptoms of acute closed-angle glaucoma
- Painful eye with signs/symptoms of chronic open-angle glaucoma
- Painful eye with signs/symptoms of infectious process
- Subjective pain without objective findings

Plan

- Loss of vision warrants immediate evaluation per physician with expedited ophthalmologic evaluation
- Chemical exposure (immediate, copious irrigation with normal saline solution per protocol)
- Do not apply pressure to globe/orbit during examination or patching if history of trauma

Think

1. *Acute angle glaucoma*: Sudden onset, photophobia, halo around lights, midsize to slightly dilated pupil, nonreactive pupil, decreased vision, central injection, tearing

2. *Iritis*: Gradual onset, severe photophobia, small pupil, central injection
3. *Temporal arteritis*: Pain around eye (specifically over course of temporal artery), loss of vision
4. *Central retinal artery or vein occlusion*: Painless loss of vision, ocular emergency
5. *Nerve entrapment*: Loss of EOMs
6. Consider possibility of cervical spine injury in any trauma above the clavicle and immobilize per protocol

VISION CHANGE/DISTURBANCE

Lisa Molitor

Subjective

- Onset and duration of symptoms
- Onset related to trauma
- Onset acute or gradual
- Use of corrective lenses (glasses or contact lenses; specify)
- Concomitant pain, especially headache or periorbital
- Concomitant tearing
- Description of change in vision (blurring, halo, scotoma, etc)
- History of hypertension
- History of previous vision problems

Objective

- See "Evaluation of Eye"
- Appearance of eye
- Periorbital swelling
- Erythema
- Tearing

- Examine for foreign body
- Examine for presence of pus or other discharge
- Evaluate for inflammation of proximal lymph nodes

Assessment

- Vision change with or without history of trauma
- Vision change with symptoms suggestive of acute glaucoma

Plan

- Stat physician evaluation if trauma, suspected acute glaucoma, obvious foreign body, or globe has been damaged
- Patch eye in interim if indicated
- Provide comfortable environment for patient with head of bed elevated, side rails up. If patient has decreased vision, do not allow independent ambulation.

Think

1. Acute glaucoma
2. Periorbital cellulitis
3. Temporal arteritis

NOSEBLEED/EPISTAXIS

Lisa Molitor

Subjective

- Onset and duration of symptoms
- Associated with trauma or spontaneous (if associated with trauma, describe mechanism of injury)

- Quantitate amount of bleeding if possible; use common household objects to help patient estimate (cup, teaspoon, etc)
- Document self-care attempted
- History of clotting dyscrasias or diseases associated with impaired coagulation (eg, liver disease)
- History of use of anticoagulants, including aspirin
- History of hypertension

Objective

- General degree of distress
- Active bleeding present (if active, is bleeding a steady flow or pulsating?)
- Clots present
- Evidence of trauma to surrounding structures, including face, mouth, orbits, cranium, cervical spine
- Evaluate blood pressure
- Examine patient for evidence of clotting dysfunction (bruising, petechiae, purpura, etc)

Assessment

- Nosebleed/epistaxis with/without active bleeding
- Nosebleed/epistaxis with/without history of trauma

Plan

- Wear protective gloves when handling patient and blood
- If actively bleeding, apply direct pressure to bridge of nose (use of gauze pad or glove may improve skin traction)
- Per physician order or protocol, ice pack may be applied to nose

- If associated with trauma, consider cervical spine immobilization
- Keep head of bed elevated
- Provide continuous oral suctioning and apply as needed
- Reassure patient as much as possible (active bleeding may cause panic)
- Monitor blood pressure if patient is hypertensive

Think

1. Traumatic injuries may not be limited to the nose; evaluate oral structures to ensure airway patency; assume cervical spine injury and immobilize per institutional/unit protocol.
2. If there is evidence of clotting impairment, examine patient carefully for other, less obvious, sites of bleeding
3. Epistaxis may be evidence of a hypertensive crisis
4. Prevent aspiration of blood

DIFFICULTY SWALLOWING

Susan Somerson
Lisa Molitor, ed.

See also "Sore Throat"

Subjective

- Onset and duration of symptoms
    1. Acute (activity immediately before onset: eating food with bones such as chicken or fish; bites/stings; ingestion of new foods)
    2. Chronic (history of URI and/or ear infection)
- Sore throat (with swallowing only or constant)
- Recent trauma to neck

- Recent stress
- Ability to swallow (water, solid food)
- Associated with neurologic symptoms suggestive of CVA
- Possible ingestion of caustic or abrasive materials
- Pertinent medical history
    1. Use of anticoagulants
    2. Use of calcium channel blockers
    3. History of scleroderma or other collagen disorder
    4. History of hemophilia
    5. History of allergies

Objective

- General appearance of patient (respiratory distress, stridor, and/or drooling
- Concomitant fever and/or lymphadenopathy
- Examination of oropharynx *(do not perform if suspicious of epiglottitis; see "Think" below)*
    1. Obvious foreign body
    2. Erythema
    3. Edema
    4. Enlarged tonsils
    5. Exudate
    6. Abscess
    7. Ulcerations
    8. Mucous membrane friability with bleeding
    9. Consider elicitation of gag reflex if appropriate
- Quality of voice (muffled or hoarse)
- Foul-smelling breath
- Head and body carriage

Assessment

- Difficulty swallowing secondary to retained foreign body or trauma arising from same

- Difficulty swallowing secondary to suspected infectious process
- Difficulty swallowing with suspected allergic response and associated edema
- Subjective difficulty swallowing without objective findings
- Potential for airway obstruction/compromise secondary to edema, hematoma, foreign body

Plan

- Expedite physician evaluation if respiratory distress is present and/or any of the following are suspected:
  1. Acute infection
  2. Epiglottitis
  3. Croup
  4. Peritonsillar abscess
  5. Retropharyngeal abscess
  6. Traumatic swelling
  7. Ingestion of caustics/abrasives
- If allergic reaction is suspected, see "Think" below
- If patient is unable to swallow secretions, have continuous suction apparatus available and monitor airway status; maintain the following equipment at the bedside: endotracheal tube, oral airway with central channel, cricothyroidotomy equipment

Think

1. Consider epiglottitis in patients aged 3 to 7 years, although epiglottitis has been reported in infants and young adults; adults may present with a less acute picture; suspect with recent history of URI, ear infection, fevers; classic physical findings include sniffing position, drooling, inspiratory stridor. *Do not agitate child in any way. Allow child to stay in parent's lap. Do not examine oropharynx or attempt to measure temperature. Allow parent to administer humidified oxygen as*

long as this does not agitate child. Arrange for immediate physician evaluation. See "Pediatric"

2. Suspect acute allergic reaction with potential for airway obstruction if history includes allergen exposure shortly before onset of symptoms followed by edema, respiratory distress, use of accessory muscles, signs of hypoxia; administer supplemental oxygen and medications (epinephrine, Benadryl) per physician order

3. Suspect oropharyngeal/airway obstruction by foreign body if symptoms have acute onset and there is drooling, respiratory distress, signs of hypoxia; provide and maintain supplemental oxygen and adjunct equipment as above (see "Plan")

SORE THROAT

Lisa Molitor

See also "Difficulty Swallowing"

Subjective

- Onset and duration of symptoms
- Concomitant fever
- Difficulty breathing
- Difficulty swallowing
- Pain with swallowing
- Tonsils present or absent
- History of trauma to neck or ingestion of caustic or abrasive substance
- Other symptoms suggestive of URI or viral illness

Objective

- Posture and breathing effort of patient, degree of distress

- Fever present
- Respiratory status (include documentation of audible breathing sounds and auscultation of lung sounds to evaluate good air exchange)
- Inspect oropharynx for injection, peritonsillar enlargement, exudate, abscess *(do not visualize throat if epiglottitis is suspected)*
- Ability to swallow (drooling evident)
- Palpation of lymph nodes (submandibular, cervical)
- "Toxic" appearance

Assessment

- Sore throat with/without evidence of systemic disease (must document respiratory status)

Plan

- Stat physician evaluation if there is respiratory compromise, drooling, or high fever, or if patient appears to be in toxic condition
- Minimize agitation if epiglottitis is suspected
- Provide for emergency suctioning of oropharynx and airway adjunct equipment as needed
- If patient has sustained trauma to neck, immobilize cervical spine per protocol

Think

1. Epiglottitis
2. Croup
3. Peritonsillar abscess
4. Retropharyngeal abscess
5. Traumatic swelling
6. Ingestion of caustic/abrasive substance

SWELLING OF ORAL STRUCTURES/SWOLLEN TONGUE

Lisa Molitor

Subjective

- Onset and duration of symptoms
- Concomitant fever, wheezing, stridor, drooling
- Associated with:
  1. Ingestion of particular food or new food
  2. Ingestion of drugs, especially newly prescribed drugs or phenothiazines
  3. Trauma to mouth, neck
- History of trauma to mouth

Objective

- General level of comfort of patient (evaluate airway and patient's ability to handle oral secretions)
- Inspect swollen area for signs of infection, trauma, bleeding

Assessment

- Swelling of region (identify region) with/without evidence of airway compromise

Plan

- Stat physician evaluation if airway is compromised or threatened
- Provide for suctioning of oropharynx if patient is drooling or choking
- Maintain adjunctive airway equipment (including tracheostomy equipment) at bedside as indicated

Think

1. Ingestion of phenothiazines
2. Acute infection/abscess
3. Traumatic swelling

NECK PAIN/STIFF NECK

Lisa Molitor

Subjective

- Onset and duration of symptoms
- Concomitant fever
- Any neurologic changes noted by patient
- History of trauma, especially deceleration injury or trauma to head
- Concomitant headache
- Concomitant chest pain or angina equivalents, with/without history of coronary artery disease
- Medications currently in use, particularly haloperidol, phenothiazines, anti-Parkinsonism agents, etc
- History of neuromuscular disease, torticollis
- History of clotting disorders, use of anticoagulants
- Associated respiratory distress

Objective

- Point tenderness
- Numbness/tingling in extremities
- Ability to ambulate
- Neurologic status (evaluate both central and peripheral)
- Upper airway status (rule out soft tissue swelling)
- Physical findings suggestive of cardiac sequelae

- Relative flexibility of neck; pain increased with flexion of neck (meningeal irritability)
- Meningeal signs (agitation/lethargy, fever, toxic appearance, opisthotonos)

Assessment

- Neck pain with/without history of trauma
- Neck pain with/without meningeal signs
- Neck stiffness with/without history of trauma
- Neck stiffness without obvious etiology

Plan

- Stat physician evaluation if patient is febrile, neurologic changes are evident, trauma to cervical spine is documented, or cardiac origin of pain is suspected

Think

1. Meningitis
2. Intracranial bleeding/lesion (can produce neck pain)
3. Cervical spine injury
4. Referred cardiac pain
5. Torticollis associated with use of phenothiazines, etc
6. Respiratory distress associated with neck trauma

HEADACHE

Lisa Molitor
Paula Turvy McCarty, ed.

Subjective

- Onset and duration of symptoms
- Generalized or localized pain

- Quantitate intensity on scale from 1 to 10, with 10 being the worst headache ever experienced
- Concomitant symptoms (nausea, vomiting, vision disturbances, neck stiffness, neck pain)
- History of trauma to head or neck
- Concomitant fever (if so, quantitate)
- History of headaches and/or migraines (if so, compare present headache to "usual" headache)
- History of toothache, dental infections, etc
- History of anticoagulant therapy or ingestion

Objective

- Level of consciousness
- Level of orientation
- Ambulatory ability
- External ocular movements
- Pupil response to light examination
- Visual acuity
- Evaluation of neck suppleness
- Presence of photophobia
- Evaluate for presence of Cushing's triad (associated with increased intracranial pressure):
  1. Bradycardia
  2. Increased systolic blood pressure
  3. Widened pulse pressure
- Quantitate apparent level of discomfort (scale of 1 to 10)
- Examine oral cavity for signs of infection, untreated caries, or other dental sources of pain

Assessment

- Headache with history of trauma, fever, hypertension, etc

- Headache with signs/symptoms of increased intracranial pressure
- Headache with meningeal signs
- Subjective headache without objective findings

Plan

- Presence of any neurologic signs warrants immediate evaluation
- Obvious discomfort warrants a comfortable waiting area
- Suspicion of infectious process warrants immediate isolation

Think

1. *Intracranial lesion:* Index of suspicion increases with history of trauma, hypertension, acute onset of symptoms, use of anticoagulants
2. *Meningitis:* Index of suspicion increases with history of fever, neck pain and/or stiffness, vomiting, gradual onset of symptoms, progression of symptoms
3. *Encephalitis:* Index of suspicion increases if fever is present or with headache associated with agitation, confusion, stupor
4. *Reye's syndrome:* Index of suspicion increases with recent viral infection, especially varicella (chickenpox) and use of salicylates; also look for vomiting, central nervous system depression, hepatic tenderness
5. *Acute glaucoma:* Associated with vision changes and pain in affected eye
6. *Increased intracranial pressure:* Associated with mental status changes in early stages; Cushing's triad signs in late stages

TOOTHACHE/JAW PAIN

Susan Somerson
Lisa Molitor, ed.

Subjective

- Onset and duration of symptoms
- Location (generalized or localized; if localized, identify area)
- Age of patient
- History of recent dental work (type, status post tooth extraction)
- Patient able to sense cold
- History of trauma to area
- History of temporomandibular joint problems
- Prior medical history (cardiovascular, hepatic, bleeding dyscrasias)
- Signs/symptoms associated with acute MI (nausea with or without vomiting, diaphoresis, shortness of breath)
- Associated fever
- Patient description of quality of pain (sharp, dull, burning); "see Evaluation of Pain"
- Presence of loose teeth
- Sensation of abnormal alignment when teeth clenched
- Recent history of URI and/or sinusitis symptoms
- Presence of nasal exudate (document color)
- Present drug therapy, particularly Dilantin, anticoagulants, aspirin

Objective

- Ensure patency of airway
- External and/or internal swelling
- Examine particularly for:
  1. Obvious decay

2. Swollen, bleeding gums
3. Ability to bite normally
4. Missing or broken teeth
5. Active bleeding or evidence of hematoma
6. Presence of gum and/or tongue lesions

- Inspect a site of recent extraction for:

    1. Edema
    2. Dry socket

- Evaluate for presence of lymphadenopathy:

    1. Submandibular
    2. Preauricular
    3. Cervical

- If patient has history of recent trauma, examine for:

    1. Occlusion
    2. Hematoma or swelling on floor of mouth, gums, oropharynx

- Document respiratory status
- Palpate over maxillary sinuses

Assessment

- Toothache (consider with/without symptoms of MI in older patients, especially with history of cardiovascular or chronic disease)
- Toothache with signs and symptoms of abscess (if patient's condition is toxic, ensure good hemodynamic status)
- Signs/symptoms of cellulitis
- Apparent mandibular/maxillary fracture/displacement
- Signs/symptoms of sinusitis
- Dental caries

Plan

- Evidence of airway compromise is of paramount concern; possible causes include:

    1. Hemorrhage, especially if accompanied by alteration in level of consciousness

    2. Edema

    3. Hematoma

    4. Loss of anatomic stability, for example flail
       mandible

- If acute MI is suspected, institute standard life support
  measures (see "Chest Pain" section for guidelines)
- If actively bleeding, apply direct pressure and provide
  for suctioning of oropharynx

Think

1. Acute MI (particularly in patients with risk factors)
   - Toothache and/or jaw pain is often associated with
     inferior MI
2. Potential for airway obstruction secondary to:
   - Soft tissue swelling over a fracture site (swelling
     may be delayed in such patients)
   - Hemorrhage, especially if accompanied by change
     in level of consciousness
   - Loose teeth moving into oropharynx or trachea, es-
     pecially if accompanied by change in level of con-
     sciousness
   - Loss of anatomic stability, particularly when there
     is obvious deformity
3. If trauma is associated with presentation, consider
   cervical spine immobilization; cervical spine injury is
   possible when trauma has occurred anywhere above
   the clavicles or with deceleration injuries

FACIAL SWELLING

Lisa Molitor

Subjective

- Onset and duration of symptoms
- Progression of symptoms (worsening over minutes,
  hours, days)

- History of trauma
- History of insect bites; exposure to allergens, chemicals, new cosmetics, new soaps or detergents, new medications
- Accompanied by palpitations and/or respiratory distress, especially wheezing
- Concomitant pain, burning, tingling
- Visual changes or eye pain
- If progression of symptoms has been greater than a few days, history of voice changes, hoarseness
- Accompanied by itching
- Ingestion of phenothiazine medications

Objective

- Quantitate degree of swelling (if unilateral, compare to unaffected side)
- Assess for wheezing or other signs of respiratory distress suggestive of allergic reaction
- Examine skin for breaks, puncture wounds, or foreign bodies consistent with insect bite
- Particularly examine tongue and oropharynx for obstructive swelling
- Particularly examine eyes for tearing, redness, pain suggestive of acute glaucoma

Assessment

- Soft tissue swelling with or without history of trauma
- Document presence or absence of respiratory distress

Plan

- If respiratory distress is present or if swelling is rapidly progressing, as with an allergic reaction, stat physician evaluation
- Support respirations as needed

- If allergic reaction in progress, anticipate some or all of the following physician orders:
  1. Oxygen
  2. Intubation equipment at bedside
  3. Continuous cardiac monitoring
  4. Epinephrine (0.01 to 0.02 mg/kg subcutaneously)
  5. Initiate intravenous access
  6. Arterial blood gas sampling
- If patient not emergently ill, urgent care designation is warranted, especially if patient is uncomfortable or if eye is involved

Think

1. Allergic reaction may rapidly progress to anaphylactic shock and/or respiratory obstruction
2. Acute glaucoma is present if swelling is periorbital and accompanied by erythema, pain, tearing
3. Phenothiazine intoxication produces extrapyramidal symptoms

Section 4

Gastrointestinal

ABDOMINAL PAIN/CRAMPING, ABDOMINAL FULLNESS, ABDOMINAL SWELLING

Lisa Molitor

Subjective

- Onset and duration of symptoms
- Trauma to abdomen (see "Abdominal Trauma")
- Associated with eating, not eating, bowel movements, change in position
- Concomitant fever
- Pain generalized or localized
- Character of pain
- Bowel movements (habits over preceding 3 days; compare with normal habits for patient, document tarry or clay-colored stools)
    1. Diarrhea (quantitate frequency, character, presence of blood and/or foul smell)
    2. Constipation (last bowel movement, accompanied by obstipation)
    3. Concomitant nausea and vomiting (if vomiting, how frequent; presence of blood)

- Previous abdominal surgeries, especially appendectomy
- Presence of hematuria, history of kidney stones
- History of gallbladder disease
- History of peptic ulcer disease
- History of Crohn's disease or other inflammatory bowel disease
- History of:
  1. Clotting disorders
  2. Previous aneurysm
  3. Recent surgery to abdomen or lower extremities
- History of liver diseases and/or ascites
- History of snake or spider bite
- History of alcohol use with/without history of pancreatitis
- Pelvic history in women (evidence or suspicion of pregnancy)
- Recent use of salicylates, nonsteroidal antiinflammatory or other drugs that can produce gastritis
- History of sickle cell disease or other blood dyscrasias

Objective

- See "Evaluation of the Abdomen"
- If patient appears ill, carefully evaluate hemodynamic status
- Presence of costo-vertebral angle tenderness
- If history of clotting disorders or evidence of aneurysm, conduct assessment of lower extremities
- If history of snake or spider bite, examine site and other systems for associated sequelae

Assessment

- Abdominal pain with/without evidence of hemodynamic compromise, infectious process, acute abdomen

Plan

- Stat physician evaluation if:
    1. Patient is hemodynamically unstable
    2. Pain is severe and/or acute
    3. Acute abdomen is suspected
    4. History of trauma
- Expedite physician evaluation if:
    1. Patient is febrile
    2. Pain is moderate
    3. Pain is accompanied by nausea and/or vomiting

Think

1. Acute gastrointestinal bleed
2. Abdominal aneurysm
3. Bowel obstruction
4. Acute appendicitis
5. Kidney stone
6. Ectopic pregnancy
7. Peritonitis, pancreatitis, or other infectious process
8. Ischemia secondary to:
    - Thromboembolism
    - Infarct of abdominal organs
9. Pelvic inflammatory disease
10. Poisonous snake bite
11. Poisonous spider bite
12. Appendicitis seldom occurs in infancy; it is most common in adolescents
13. Obstruction of the large intestine by cancerous stricture is seldom seen before 30 years of age and infrequently before 40, but it is the most common cause of obstruction in persons older than 40 years of age
14. Acute pancreatitis is seldom seen in young adults unless there is a long history of alcohol abuse
15. The following conditions have been reported to masquerade sometimes as an abdominal disorder, especially when pain is located in the upper quadrants:

- Intrathoracic infection or inflammation or pneumothorax
- Myocardial ischemia, infarct, or infection
- Esophageal disorders

BIBLIOGRAPHY

Cope Z. *The Early Diagnosis of the Acute Abdomen*. London: Oxford University Press; 1972:48-78.

BLOOD IN STOOL

Lisa Molitor
Susan Somerson, ed.

Subjective

- Onset and duration of symptoms
- Bright red, dark red, or tarry stool
- Quantitate if possible; document clots
- Continuous oozing or present only with bowel movement
- Previous history
- History of Crohn's disease, ulcerative colitis, diverticulitis, diverticulosis, ulcer disease
- Pain localized to anus, rectum, abdominal area; pain on bearing down to have bowel movement
- History of foreign body in rectum or trauma
- History of hemorrhoids
- Concomitant diarrhea, obstipation, constipation, vomiting
- Recent weight loss
- Associated fevers
- Report of appetite
- Report of indigestion and/or pain with eating

- History of ingestion of caustics, alcohol
- In female patients, question about possibility that bleeding is actually originating from vagina or urethra
- Use of medications *(Note: medications containing iron or bismuth, including Pepto-Bismol, will sometimes produce dark, tarry stools that are not related to gastrointestinal bleeding)*

Objective

- Immediate evaluation of hemodynamic status
- Visualize perineum if possible
- Gently examine abdomen to rule out emergent vascular sequelae

Assessment

- Rectal bleeding with/without evidence of hemodynamic compromise
- History of rectal bleeding with/without evidence of active bleeding

Plan

- Stat physician evaluation if hemodynamically unstable and/or actively bleeding
- Obtain stool sample if clinical status indicates (guaiac)
- Guaiac any emesis
- If infectious process is suspected (bloody diarrhea with or without fever), implement enteric isolation

Think

1. Acute gastrointestinal bleed
2. Gastrointestinal infection

CHANGE IN BOWEL HABITS (CONSTIPATION/ OBSTIPATION, BLOOD IN STOOL)

Lisa Molitor

See also "Diarrhea"

Subjective

- Onset and duration of symptoms
- Change is:
    1. Constipation/obstipation
    2. Blood in stool
    3. Color of stool (clay-colored, tarry)
    4. Diarrhea (see "Diarrhea")
- Concomitant pain (see also "Rectal Pain")
- If blood in stool, history of clotting dyscrasias, leukemia, thrombocytopenia, etc
- History of Crohn's disease, ulcerative colitis, diverticulosis/diverticulitis, or other gastrointestinal illness
- Recent exposure to high residue substances in diet or drastic change in diet

Objective

- Evaluate for signs of acute abdomen
- If acute abdomen is suspected, if patient is febrile, if patient reports blood in stool, or if patient reports diarrhea that may have produced dehydration, evaluate hemodynamic status
- Guaiac any stool present

Assessment

- Change in bowel habits (specify) with/without evidence of:

1. Acute abdomen
2. Gastrointestinal bleeding
3. Hemodynamic instability
4. Severe pain

Plan

- Stat physician evaluation if any of the following are present:
    1. Acute abdomen
    2. Hemodynamic instability
    3. Fever
    4. Pain
- Obtain stool specimen, if possible

Think

1. Acute gastrointestinal bleed
2. Acute abdomen

DIARRHEA

Lisa Molitor

Subjective

- Onset and duration of symptoms
- Concomitant nausea, vomiting
- Concomitant pain
- Concomitant fever
- Character of stools (consistency, frequency, color, foul odor)
- If diarrhea is long term, subjective signs/symptoms of dehydration

- History of exposure to gastrointestinal infection (housemates with similar symptoms, recent intake of unsanitized water, recent travel to primitive locales)
- Use of liquid diet preparations
- Exposure to pesticides, herbicides
- Medication used, particularly antibiotics, antacids, H_2 blockers, laxatives, xanthines
- History of thyroid disorders (thyrotoxicosis)

Objective

- General degree of distress
- Hemodynamic assessment, orthostatic vital signs
- Temperature assessment
- If patient appears to be in toxic condition or in pain, evaluate abdomen
- If stool sample available, document consistency and color, guaiac

Assessment

- Acute or chronic diarrhea with/without evidence of dehydration
- Acute or chronic diarrhea with/without evidence of infectious process

Plan

- If hemodynamically compromised, expedite evaluation per physician
- If infectious process is suspected, provide for enteric isolation
- Monitor vital signs frequently, per departmental protocol
- Obtain stool sample

Think

1. Gastrointestinal infection
2. Appendicitis
3. Hypovolemia secondary to dehydration with/without electrolyte/acid-base disturbance

RECTAL PAIN

Lisa Molitor

Subjective

- Onset and duration of symptoms
- Evaluation of pain
- Accompanied by change in bowel habits, particularly rectal bleeding (document occurrence and character of bowel movements in previous 24 hours or whenever last bowel movement occurred)
- History of rectal trauma and/or foreign body
- Radiation of pain to abdomen, back, groin
- Accompanied by fever
- History of Crohn's disease, ulcerative colitis, diverticulosis/diverticulitis, hemorrhoids

Objective

- Evaluation of hemodynamic status, if warranted
- Guaiac stool if present
- Evaluate abdomen

Assessment

- Rectal pain with/without history of trauma
- Rectal pain with/without evidence of rectal bleeding

Plan

- Provide comfort measures, particularly positioning
- Anticipate some or all of the following physician orders:
  1. Abdomen supine and erect radiographs
  2. Guaiac stools
  3. Complete blood count with differential
  4. Enema

Think

1. Abdominal aneurysm
2. If trauma has occurred and/or there is bleeding, consider rupture of viscus organ
3. Perirectal abscess
4. Obstipation producing lower bowel obstruction
5. Occult trauma/abuse in children and elderly or disabled patients
6. Occult foreign body

**THROWING UP BLOOD,
SPITTING UP BLOOD,
COUGHING UP BLOOD**

Lisa Molitor

Note: If patient is bleeding from nose, producing apparent hemoptysis, see "Nosebleed/Epistaxis"

Subjective

- Onset and duration of symptoms
- Ascertain whether apparent source of blood is gastrointestinal tract, lungs, or oropharynx (patient may be unsure)
- Associated with syncope, presyncope, dizziness, shortness of breath

- Character of blood (bright red, dark, clotted, free-flowing)
- Quantity of blood (use common household objects to estimate such as cup, teaspoon, etc)
- Body weight stable, loss, or gain
- Use of anticoagulant medications
- History of clotting disorders, leukemia, thrombocytopenia, etc
- History of trauma to face, mouth, neck, chest, or abdomen, including foreign bodies
- If vomiting blood (hematemesis):
    1. Accompanied by pain (chest, upper abdomen, lower abdomen)
    2. Associated with change in bowel habits (bright red blood per rectum, dark tarry stools, diarrhea)
    3. Associated with change in eating habits
    4. Associated weight loss
- If spitting blood (ie, source in oropharyngeal cavity):
    1. Associated with infection or trauma to face, mouth, neck, or oral cavity
- If coughing up blood (hemoptysis):
    1. Concomitant shortness of breath
    2. Chest pain
    3. Cough
    4. Weight loss
    5. History of tuberculosis
    6. History of neoplasm
    7. History of other respiratory diseases, such as cystic fibrosis, COPD, fungal infections, pulmonary edema, etc
    8. History of cardiac disorders, such as mitral valve stenosis, congestive heart failure, etc

Objective

- Careful evaluation of hemodynamic status with orthostatic vital signs is essential

- Assess respiratory status in patients who are experiencing hemoptysis and/or bleeding from oropharynx, especially if associated with trauma
- Inspect oropharynx and nares for evidence of trauma and/or active bleeding

Assessment

- Hemoptysis with apparent site of bleeding in:
  1. Oropharynx
  2. Gastrointestinal tract
  3. Respiratory tract
- History of hemoptysis without active bleeding

Note: Some authors refer to bleeding from the oropharynx or gastrointestinal tract as pseudohemoptysis, reserving the term hemoptysis for bleeding from the respiratory tract

Plan

- If hemodynamic compromise, expedite physician evaluation and provide appropriate supportive interventions
- If respiratory compromise, expedite physician evaluation and provide appropriate supportive interventions
- Implement respiratory isolation if tuberculosis or other infectious respiratory disease is suspected
- Provide for oropharyngeal suctioning if there is active bleeding
- Implement enteric isolation if gastrointestinal infection is suspected
- May obtain sputum sample per departmental protocol
- Do not dislodge any clots that may be present as long as airway is not obstructed

Think

1. Pulmonary edema
2. Mallory-Weiss tear
3. Acute gastrointestinal bleed resulting in hypovolemic shock
4. Trauma to face/nose may put airway at risk, immobilize cervical spine
5. Prevent aspiration of blood

VOMITING

Lisa Molitor

Subjective

- Onset and duration of symptoms
- Character of emesis (frequency, consistency, presence of blood or bilious material)
- Concomitant diarrhea, abdominal pain, fever
- Bowel activity (increased, decreased, absent)
- "Flu" symptoms (malaise, aching, etc)
- Possible pregnancy (hyperemesis gravidarum)
- Recent viral syndrome with/without use of salicylates
- Recent headaches and/or head trauma
- Recent ear infection
- Concomitant vertigo, dizziness
- Possible exposure to toxins, especially pesticides or heavy metals
- Use of:
    1. Aminophylline/xanthine
    2. Digitalis
    3. Alcohol
    4. Chemotherapeutic agents
    5. Anticholinergic drugs

- History of previous abdominal surgery, abdominal trauma, or bowel obstruction
- History of gastrointestinal disorder
- History of diabetes

Objective

- If vomiting has been severe and/or prolonged or has been accompanied by diarrhea, evaluate for signs/symptoms of dehydration, including orthostatic vital signs
- If emesis has contained blood, conduct hemodynamic examination
- Abdominal examination
- General appearance (note presence of fever or toxic appearance)

Assessment

- Vomiting with/without symptoms of:
  1. Dehydration
  2. Possible bowel obstruction
  3. "Flu"
  4. Concomitant diarrhea

Plan

- Expedite care if patient has orthostatic vital sign changes, hematemesis, or symptoms consistent with one of the conditions listed under "Think" below

Think

1. Reye's syndrome
2. Bowel obstruction
3. Acute abdomen

4. Hyperemesis gravidarum
5. Dehydration
6. Increased intracranial pressure
7. Meniere's syndrome (do not allow patient to attempt ambulation because of danger of falling)
8. Mallory-Weiss tear (suspect if patient reports hematemesis, particularly if vomiting has been protracted and/or forceful)
9. Diabetic ketoacidosis in patients with known diabetes; also consider possibility of previously undiagnosed diabetes
10. Gastrointestinal infection if vomiting is accompanied by diarrhea
11. Altitude sickness

Section 5

Genitourinary

DYSURIA, BURNING ON URINATION

Lisa Molitor

Subjective

- Onset and duration of symptoms
- Report of:
    1. Frequency
    2. Pain
    3. Urgency
    4. Back pain
    5. Abdominal pain
    6. Fever, chills
    7. Cloudy, foul-smelling urine
    8. Hematuria
- Concomitant vaginal or penile discharge
- History of previous urinary tract infections
- History of renal stones
- Fluid intake recently; history of vomiting with onset of symptoms

- Estimate of amount voided with each void and/or over the course of the day (symptoms of urinary obstruction present)
- General state of health, particularly immunosuppression
- In women, possible pregnancy (question women carefully; many antibiotics are contraindicated in pregnancy)
- In men, history of prostatic enlargement, prostatitis

Objective

- General degree of distress
- Toxic appearance
- Febrile
- Presence of CVA tenderness
- Abbreviated abdominal examination if complaints include abdominal pain, with special consideration to distended bladder
- Urine dipstick results

Assessment

- Dysuria with:
  1. Fever
  2. Hematuria
  3. Bladder distension
- Dysuria without objective findings

Plan

- Obtain clean catch specimen for U/A, culture, and sensitivity per physician order or unit protocol
- Expedite care if patient is in great distress or in toxic condition and/or febrile, or if bladder is distended

Think

1. If patient appears in a toxic condition or febrile with/ without evidence of dehydration, conduct hemodynamic assessment
2. If bladder is distended, patient may have urinary obstruction

PELVIC PAIN (FEMALES)

Lisa Molitor

See also "Suprapubic Pain", "Abdominal Pain"

Subjective

- Onset and duration of symptoms
- Symptoms progressive or static in nature
- Generalized or localized (if localized, at what site)
- Concomitant fever, vaginal bleeding or discharge, pain with intercourse, change in bowel habits, change in bladder habits
- Presence or absence of back pain (document specifically)
- Use of contraceptives, particularly intrauterine device
- Menstrual history; pregnancy possible
- History of trauma

Objective

- Hemodynamic status if patient appears in toxic condition and/or is febrile
- Assessment of abdomen to include auscultation for bruit
- If vaginal or rectal bleeding or perineal trauma is reported, visualize perineum if possible
- Evaluate CVA tenderness

- If trauma has been sustained, evaluate stability of pelvic cradle if fractured pelvis is suspected

Assessment

- Pelvic pain with/without evidence of acute abdomen
- Pelvic pain with/without evidence of hemodynamic compromise

Plan

- Stat physician evaluation if patient appears in toxic condition or is hemodynamically unstable
- Obtain urine for dipstick evaluation; use clean-catch method or catheterize (send culture and U/A if protocol allows)
- Start pad count if vaginal bleeding is present

Think

1. Dissecting aortic aneurysm
2. Sepsis related to pyelonephritis or pelvic inflammatory disease
3. Acute abdomen, including but not limited to appendicitis
4. Inevitable abortion
5. Pelvic fracture if patient has sustained trauma

PENILE DISCHARGE

Lisa Molitor

Subjective

- Onset and duration of symptoms
- Character of discharge

  1. Color
  2. Consistency
  3. Bleeding present
- Concomitant pain
  1. Location (radiation to abdomen and/or testicles)
  2. Duration
- History of trauma
  1. Direct
  2. Indirect
  3. Foreign body in urethra
- Systemic symptoms
  1. Fever
  2. Difficulty urinating
- Psychosexual history
  1. Last intercourse
  2. Known contact with person with STD
  3. History of STD

Objective

- General level of distress
- Examine penis if patient reports:
  1. Severe distress
  2. History of trauma
  3. Foreign body in urethra
  4. Bleeding
- If dysuria is present and patient has been unable to void well, examine bladder for possible distension

Assessment

   Penile discharge with/without history of trauma, possible exposure to STD, fever, dysuria

Plan

- Stat physician evaluation if:
  1. Penis has been traumatized and obvious deformity or bleeding is present or if foreign body is present

2. Associated dysuria has caused distended bladder
3. Patient is febrile and appears in toxic condition
4. Patient is in severe pain or distress
5. Testicular symptoms are reported

- Obtain urine specimen (do not catheterize before physician evaluation)

Think

1. Penile trauma
2. Foreign body
3. Abuse in children or elderly or incapacitated patients

PUBIC/SUPRAPUBIC PAIN

Lisa Molitor

Determine precise location of pain. If pain is located in abdomen, refer to "Abdominal Pain." If pain is located in pubis and/or suprapubic region, see below.

Subjective

- Onset and duration of symptoms
- Character of pain
- Pain localized or generalized (if localized, identify site)
- Pain radiating to back, testicle(s)
- Concomitant:
    1. Fever
    2. Dysuria
    3. Report of frequent, small-volume voiding
    4. Hematuria
    5. Change in bowel habits (describe)
- History of trauma to region
- History of renal stones or other obstructive conditions

Objective

- Evaluate general level of distress
- Examine abdomen for breaks in skin, erythema, ecchymosis, etc
- Auscultate all four quadrants for bowel sounds and presence of bruit
- Palpate iliac crests for evidence of skeletal instability
- Palpate abdomen to check for bladder distension

Assessment

- Pubic/suprapubic pain with/without evidence of:
    1. Gastrointestinal sequelae
    2. Genitourinary sequelae
    3. Trauma to region
    4. Hemodynamic instability

Plan

- Stat physician evaluation if:
    1. Pain is severe
    2. Patient is hemodynamically unstable
    3. Abdomen is distended
    4. Bladder is distended
    5. Status post trauma to area
    6. Skeletal instability is present
    7. Evidence of aneurysm is present (abdominal bruit)

Think

1. Bowel obstruction
2. Pelvic fracture (suspect if there is history of trauma, particularly straddle injury)
3. Abdominal aneurysm
4. Torsion of testicle if pain radiates to scrotum
5. Bowel abscess, diverticulitis

TESTICULAR PAIN/GROIN PAIN

Lisa Molitor

Subjective

- Onset and duration of symptoms
- Related to trauma
- Concomitant fever
- Hematuria
- History of kidney stones
- History of inguinal/femoral hernia
- Concomitant penile discharge
- Swelling or erythema present
- General statement of health

Objective

- General degree of distress
- Examine area if:
  1. Patient is in severe distress
  2. There is history of trauma
  3. Foreign body in urethra is suspected
  4. There is report of bleeding
  5. There is report of swelling
  6. Incarcerated inguinal hernia is suspected
  7. Patient is febrile
- If dysuria is present and patient has been unable to void well, examine bladder for possible distension

Assessment

- Testicular pain with/without history of trauma
- Testicular pain with/without evidence of infectious process

Plan

- Immediate physician evaluation is warranted for acute testicular pain
- Position patient as comfortably as possible
- Obtain urine specimen (do not catheterize before physician evaluation)
- Apply ice compress to traumatized area per physician order

Think

1. Occult trauma, especially in children and elderly or impaired patients
2. Torsion of testicle
3. Incarcerated inguinal hernia
4. Kidney stones

VAGINAL BLEEDING

Lisa Molitor

Subjective

- Onset and duration of symptoms
- Document last normal menses in child-bearing age group (if pregnancy suspected, estimate date of conception and gestational dates from menstrual history)
- Document child-bearing history (full-term deliveries, premature deliveries, abortions, living children)
- Document severity of bleeding (number of pads and/or tampons used per hour)
- Have patient distinguish stained pad from soaked pad
- Presence of clots
- Bright red or dark brown blood

- History of unprotected intercourse; document whether patient suspects pregnancy
- Presence of intrauterine device
- Use of oral contraceptives
- Concomitant abdominal pain
- Concomitant fever
- History of vaginal/perineal trauma
- History of clotting dyscrasias, thrombocytopenia, leukemia, etc
- History of heavy aspirin or anticoagulant medication use

Objective

- Orthostatic blood pressure and pulse measurement
- If possible, examine perineum to estimate ongoing blood loss and to ensure that bleeding is from vagina and not other tissue
- Evaluate abdomen as indicated

Assessment

- Vaginal bleeding with/without evidence of hemodynamic compromise
- History of vaginal bleeding without active bleeding

Plan

- Stat physician evaluation if significant orthostatic changes noted in pulse/blood pressure
- Stat physician evaluation if spontaneous abortion is suspected (especially after first trimester) or if tissue is present at introitus
- Start pad count
- Save any tissue that may be passed
- Stat physician evaluation if significant abdominal pain (other than menstrual cramping) is present, if patient is

in postpartum period, or if patient has a known pregnancy of more than 16 weeks

Think

1. Inevitable abortion
2. Ectopic pregnancy (usually accompanied by significant, well-localized abdominal pain)
3. Pelvic inflammatory disease (usually accompanied by fever and generalized abdominal pain, sometimes accompanied by dark red vaginal bleeding)
4. Laceration or other trauma to vagina, perineum, cervix, or anal/rectal tissues
5. Postpartum infection or retained products of conception

VAGINAL DISCHARGE

Lisa Molitor

Subjective

- Onset and duration of symptoms
- Character of discharge:
    1. Consistency
    2. Color
    3. Odor
    4. Blood (quantitate amount of blood; if significant, see "Vaginal Bleeding")
- History of previous discharges, infections, neoplasms
- Is patient sexually active
- Possible pregnancy
- Recent abortion
- Date of last menstrual period
- Type of contraception used
- Discharge accompanied by pain/discomfort:

1. Perineal
2. Vaginal
3. Abdominal
4. With intercourse

- History of fever
- General statement of health (ask particularly about diabetes mellitus, immunosuppression)

Objective

- Relative degree of distress
- If patient appears in toxic condition, conduct hemodynamic assessment
- Abdominal examination to rule out acute abdomen if patient is febrile or in severe pain, has a toxic appearance, or has a possible ectopic pregnancy

Assessment

- Vaginal discharge with/without:
    1. Fever
    2. Abdominal pain
    3. Vaginal bleeding
    4. Suspected/known pregnancy

Plan

- Stat physician evaluation if acute abdomen is suspected, if patient appears in toxic condition, or if vaginal bleeding is significant
- Expedite evaluation if patient is febrile or in distress

Think

1. Acute abdomen secondary to pelvic inflammatory disease
2. Missed spontaneous abortion
3. Sepsis related to infection

Section 6

Miscellaneous

ASYMMETRY OF SHOULDER/CHEST

Lisa Molitor

Subjective

- Onset and duration of symptoms (associated with trauma)
- Concomitant pain at site of deformity
- Concomitant pain with inspiration/expiration
- Subjective shortness of breath, dyspnea

Objective

- Respiratory status (respiratory rate, depth of respiration, presence of breath sounds, comparison of breath sounds across thorax to ensure equality and good air exchange, presence of cyanosis in periphery
- Document presence and quality of upper extremity pulses and compare to lower extremity pulses
- Position of trachea (at midline)
- Concomitant swelling of soft tissues of head and neck
- Evaluate for jugular vein distension, gallop, muffled heart sounds

Assessment

- Shoulder or chest (specify) asymmetry with/without history of trauma to area
- Shoulder or chest (specify) asymmetry with/without evidence of respiratory sequelae

Plan

- Stat physician evaluation if:
  1. Evidence of respiratory sequelae present
  2. Evidence of neurovascular compromise present
- Expedite physician evaluation if:
  1. Pain is severe
  2. Obvious deformity present
- Splint shoulder or upper arm with sling and swath per unit protocol

Think

1. Pneumothorax, especially tension pneumothorax
2. Fracture clavicle, putting patient at risk for pneumothorax
3. Shoulder dislocation, with possible loss of blood supply

BACK PAIN

Lisa Molitor

Subjective

- Onset and duration of symptoms
- Location
- Associated with trauma
- Referred to back from chest and/or abdomen

- Presence of CVA tenderness
- Associated symptoms of urinary tract infection
- Associated gastrointestinal symptoms, especially abdominal pain, rectal bleeding, and/or constipation
- Concomitant symptoms of bowel obstruction
- Loss of motor and/or sensory function in any extremity
- Loss of bowel or bladder control
- History of scoliosis, lordosis, kyphosis
- History of arthritis
- Ability to ambulate

Objective

- Assess for neurologic findings in all extremities
- Assess for presence of abdominal bruit; document presence or absence
- Assess pulses in all extremities (optional : assess blood pressure in all extremities)
- Assess for presence of CVA tenderness

Assessment

- Back pain with/without evidence of:
    1. Neurologic deficit
    2. Hemodynamic instability
- Back pain with associated symptoms:
    1. Gastrointestinal symptoms
    2. Urinary/nephrotic symptoms
    3. Pain radiating to abdomen

Plan

- If neurologic deficit present, stat physician evaluation

- If associated with trauma, especially direct trauma or shearing trauma, consider immobilization and obtain immediate physician evaluation
- If evidence of hemodynamic instability present, initiate appropriate resuscitation efforts and stat physician evaluation

Think

1. Aortic aneurysm
2. Fracture of vertebral bodies with actual or potential injury to spinal cord
3. Patients experiencing difficulty or pain with ambulation should be assisted with wheelchair to prevent falls
4. Common sources of referred back pain:
   - Hip
   - Pelvis
   - Retroperitoneum (hematoma)
   - Kidneys
   - Abdominal organs
   - Heart
   - Pulmonary structures (pulmonary embolism, pleuritis, pneumonitis)

BREAST: LUMP, PAIN, DISCHARGE FROM NIPPLE

Lisa Molitor

Subjective

- Onset and duration of symptoms
- Associated with trauma
- Document whether patient is currently or recently breastfeeding or in immediate postpartum period
- Concomitant fever
- History of tumors, fibrocystic disease

- If discharge present, describe character of discharge:
  1. Color
  2. Consistency
  3. Odor
  4. Amount

Objective

- Evaluate general degree of distress
- Evaluate for evidence of infectious process
- Examine breast for evidence of trauma
- Optional: Palpate lymph nodes for evidence of inflammation

Assessment

- Pain in breast/nipple (specify site) with/without history of trauma
- Pain in breast/nipple (specify site) with/without evidence of infection
- Pain in breast/nipple (specify site) in lactating patient

Plan

- Initiate comfort measures as indicated
- Expedite physician evaluation if patient is febrile, appears in toxic condition, or is in severe distress

CHANGE IN COLOR OF SKIN: GENERALIZED OR LOCALIZED (JAUNDICE, FLUSHING, PALLOR, CYANOSIS)

Lisa Molitor

Subjective

- Onset and duration of symptoms

- Concomitant symptoms present

Objective

- Color change is:
    1. Flushing (erythema)
    2. Jaundice
    3. Pallor
    4. Cyanosis
    5. Generalized
    6. Localized

Assessment

- Skin color change with or without evidence of systemic sequelae

Plan

- Interventions are based on suspected cause of color change

FEVER

Lisa Molitor

Distinguish fever from hyperthermia. If hyperthermic state is suspected, arrange stat physician evaluation.

Subjective

- Onset and duration of symptoms
- Concomitant symptoms (thorough assessment to include brief review of systems):

1. "Flu" symptoms
2. Shortness of breath, dyspnea, cough
3. Abdominal pain
4. Joint or extremity pain
5. Dysuria
6. Headache
7. Neck stiffness/meningeal signs (see "Neck Pain")

- History of trauma

- Temperature measured or "tactile" fever (if measured, document degree and time)

- Pattern of fever (varying throughout day, increased at night)

- Careful assessment of medications (any and all antipyretics taken, including dose, frequency, and time last dose taken; also ask carefully about any other medications currently in use)

- Recent insect bite, particularly tick bite

- Accompanied by rash, lymphadenopathy, neurologic sequelae, muscle/joint aches, and/or weakness

Objective

- General assessment to emphasize signs/symptoms of dehydration and/or hemodynamic instability

- Evaluate for presence of rashes, skin lesions, or other breaks in the skin, including needle marks

- Lymph node enlargement and tenderness

- Respiratory auscultation to rule out major pneumonia, empyema, upper airway infection

Assessment

- Fever with/without evidence of hemodynamic compromise

- Fever with evidence of toxic process and/or infectious process

Think

1. *Dehydration associated with fever and febrile illness*
2. *Sepsis with/without shock*
3. *Acute infectious disease, including AIDS, Lyme disease, meningitis:* isolate per unit policy
4. *Drug-induced fever:* Fever most often represents an inflammatory and/or infectious process, but without obvious localizing signs/symptoms may be associated with the use of certain medications:

- Antihistamines
- Barbiturates
- Bleomycin
- Carbamazepine
- Cephalosporins
- Cimetadine
- Hydralazine
- Ibuprofen
- Iodides
- Methyldopa
- Nifedipine
- Nitrofurantoin
- Phenytoin
- Penicillins
- Procainamide
- Quinidine
- Rifampin
- Salicylates
- Streptozocin
- Sulfonamides

BIBLIOGRAPHY

Kinkinson CA, Brusch JL, Fitzgerald FT. How to evaluate patients having fever without localizing signs or symptoms. *Emerg Med Rep.* 1989;10.

Mackowiak PA, LeMaustre CF. Drug fever: a critical appraisal of conventional concepts. *Ann Intern Med.* 1987;106.

"FLU" SYMPTOMS

Lisa Molitor

Subjective

- Onset and duration of symptoms
- General state of health (patients who are immunocompromised and the very young and very old are at high risk for complications with viral syndromes)
- Symptoms reported (symptoms can be evaluated as outlined in other sections of the text):
    1. Vomiting (amount and frequency)
    2. Diarrhea (amount and frequency)
    3. Headache (rate severity on scale from 1 to 10)
    4. Malaise
    5. Joint pains (generalized or localized)
    6. Fever (quantitate if possible)
    7. Rhinorrhea
    8. Cough (productive)
- Recent exposure to others with similar symptoms
- Presence of neurologic sequelae, especially if patient has been using salicylates

Objective

- General degree of distress
- If condition is toxic, conduct hemodynamic assessment
- If respiratory symptoms are present, conduct respiratory assessment
- If headache is present, assess for neck pain, rigidity
- Examine patient for rash, petechiae, purpura, lymphadenopathy

Assessment

- Flulike symptoms with/without evidence of hemodynamic compromise

- Flulike symptoms with/without fever

Plan

- Stat physician evaluation if any of the following are present:
    1. Hemodynamic instability
    2. High fever
    3. Meningeal signs or neurologic changes
    4. Petechiae, purpura
- Implement isolation per unit policy if infectious disease is suspected

Think

1. Dehydration associated with symptoms
2. Meningitis
3. Reye's syndrome

LUMPS/LOCALIZED SWELLING

Lisa Molitor

Subjective

- Onset and duration of symptoms
- Site of swelling
- Concomitant fever
- General statement of health and wellness, especially history of immunosuppression
- Swollen area painful
- Recent exposure to infectious disease
- Recent animal or insect bite
- History of leukemia or other neoplasms
- History of clotting dyscrasias

- History of allergen exposure if swelling is in face, throat, or neck

Objective

- Swelling located in proximity of lymph nodes or other tissues
- Character of swelling (discrete, matted, diffuse)
- Estimate size of swelling, document size and location
- Tenderness elicited
- If cervical, submandibular, or preauricular, ensure airway patency
- Presence of petechiae, purpura
- Palpate lymph chains for further involvement
- Document presence of fever, tachycardia, hypotension
- If appearance is toxic, evaluate hemodynamic status
- Careful evaluation of respiratory status as indicated

Assessment

- Lymphadenopathy with/without toxic appearance
- Localized swelling in (specify region)

   Note: If swelling involves head, ear, eye, nose, or throat area, document airway patency.

Plan

- Stat physician evaluation if any of the following are present:
   1. Involved or potentially involved airway
   2. Toxic appearance
   3. Hemodynamic instability
   4. History of leukemia or immunosuppression
   5. Presence of petechiae, purpura

6. High fever

- Institute appropriate isolation protocols (based on unit/institutional policy) if there is evidence of infectious disease and/or immunosuppression (reverse isolation)

Think

1. Acute infection
2. AIDS
3. Tumor
4. Abscess
5. New-onset leukemia
6. Acute hemodynamic compromise secondary to sepsis
7. Acute respiratory compromise secondary to anatomic obstruction of airway

RASH

Lisa Molitor

Subjective

- Onset and duration of symptoms
- Generalized or localized (if localized, describe pattern)
- Associated with fever, urticaria, lymphadenopathy
- Hematuria present
- Recent exposure to person(s) with similar rash
- Associated with respiratory distress

Objective

- If patient appears in toxic condition, conduct thorough assessment of respiratory and hemodynamic status
- Macular or papular rash vesicles, eroded

- Lesions weeping (if yes, describe exudate)
- Accompanied by petechiae and/or purpura

Assessment

- Primary differentiations to be made in triage area :
    1. Whether rash is likely to be infectious
    2. Whether rash is associated with respiratory or he-
       modynamic sequelae

Plan

- Stat physician evaluation if patient is hemodynamically compromised, has high fever, or appears in toxic
  condition
- Institute isolation per protocol

Think

1. Waterhouse-Friderichsen syndrome (purpura, hypotension, vascular collapse, and visceral hemorrhage resulting from septicemia and production of
   endotoxins)
2. Petechiae and/or purpura should be considered a serious finding; various contagious and noncontagious
   but serious illnesses produce petechiae and purpura;
   a patient with either should be evaluated by a physician immediately.
3. Quick but careful evaluation of hemodynamic status
   is warranted.

Note: Meningococcemia and Hemophilus influenzae
*septicemia may produce petechiae or purpura; the pa-
tient with a toxic appearance, fever, and/or meningeal
signs should be considered emergently ill; meningococcemia and* H influenzae *infections may produce fulminant
shock rapidly,*[1-3] *especially in children*

REFERENCES

1. Cosgriff JH, Anderson AL. *The Practice of Emergency Care*. Philadelphia: Lippincott; 1984:480-483.

2. Molitor L. A child with fever and purpura. *J Emerg Nurs*. 1988;14:118-119

3. Wintrobe, et al. *Harrison's Principles of Internal Medicine*. New York: McGraw-Hill; 1982:786, 815, 1804.

SWEATING

Lisa Molitor

Subjective

- Onset and duration of symptoms
- General state of health, with particular attention to history of tuberculosis, AIDS, infectious diseases
- History of diabetes or hypoglycemia; last food eaten
- Concomitant fever
- Concomitant pain
- Concomitant weakness/dizziness
- Other symptoms associated:
  1. Rash
  2. Lymph node enlargement
  3. Bruising
  4. Chest pain
  5. Shortness of breath
  6. Weakness
- Related to exertion or while at rest
- Recent exposure to infectious disease
- Concomitant gastrointestinal symptoms
- History of cardiac disease
- Onset at particular time of day (ie, "night sweats")
- Presence of angina equivalents

Objective

- If patient is febrile and/or hypotensive and/or cardiac condition is suspected, conduct cardiovascular assessment, including evaluation for orthostasis
- Presence of bruising and/or petechiae
- Presence of lymphadenopathy
- If patient reports respiratory symptoms, conduct respiratory assessment
- Consider Chemstick glucose measurement per unit/institutional protocol

Assessment

- History of diaphoresis with/without evidence of hemodynamic compromise
- Currently diaphoretic, hemodynamically stable/unstable

Plan

- Stat physician evaluation if evidence of:
    1. Hemodynamic compromise
    2. Cardiac event

Think

1. Shock will produce cold, clammy skin; sepsis, sometimes known as warm shock, may produce hyperdynamic state in early stages
2. Vasovagal episodes will often produce diaphoresis
3. Hypoglycemia
4. "Night sweats" may be associated with tuberculosis and AIDS; consider appropriate isolation
5. Diaphoresis may be a manifestation of angina, especially in patients with neuropathies (eg, diabetics)

WEAKNESS

Lisa Molitor

See also "Dizziness/Syncope"

Subjective

- Onset and duration of symptoms
- Determine whether patient is generally weak or whether weakness is limited to specific locale (if generally weak, differentiate symptoms from dizziness/syncope)
- Location of symptoms:
  1. Generalized
  2. Localized
     —To face (specific site)
     —To extremities (one extremity or more than one)
- Accompanied by:
  1. Color change
  2. Respiratory distress, particularly tachypnea
  3. Loss of motor control (in face or extremities)
  4. Pain in proximal area
  5. Chest pain
- Associated with trauma to area
- History of:
  1. Long-term alcohol use
  2. Diabetes mellitus
  3. Hypoglycemia
  4. Chronic anemia
  5. Recent viral syndrome
  6. Recent immunization
  7. Recent cat or dog bite or scratch
  8. Possible exposure to ticks
  9. Previous CVA
  10. Use of anticoagulants
  11. Clotting disorders or coagulopathies
  12. AIDS

Objective

- Quantitate general level of distress
- If facial numbness, evaluate cranial nerves
- If facial, evaluate for motor sensory integrity in extremities
- If facial, evaluate level of consciousness
- If localized, examine site for neurovascular integrity
- If extremity, carry out thorough examination
- Assess ability to ambulate, compare lower extremity function to upper extremity function (many progressive neurologic illnesses progress from distal to proximal), assess ability to stand from sitting position (if ambulatory)
- Concomitant respiratory distress related to neuromuscular symptoms (inability to expand chest)
- Assess for drooling (CVA and demyelinating disease may put patient at risk for aspiration or choking)

Assessment

- Weakness with/without adequate respiratory effort
- Weakness associated with head, neck, or extremity trauma
- Generalized weakness without apparent cause
- Localized weakness (specify site) with/without normal neurovascular status

Plan

- Expedite physician evaluation if:
  1. Evidence of respiratory compromise
  2. Mental status changes present
- Do not allow patient to ambulate independently

Think

1. Demyelinating disease
2. Guillain-Barré syndrome, myasthenia gravis
3. Hyperventilation syndrome (determine why patient is hyperventilating)
4. CVA
5. Thromboembolus to peripheral structure
6. Nerve damage due to direct trauma or traumatic swelling
7. Lyme disease
8. Hypoglycemia
9. Potential for aspiration or choking if patient is unable to swallow or protect airway

Section 7

Neurologic

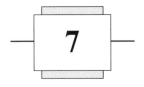

ATAXIA

Lisa Molitor

Subjective

- Onset and duration of symptoms
- Concomitant neurologic sequelae (change in level of consciousness, altered mental status)
- Concomitant pain (headache, joint pain)
- History of neurologic problems
- History of head trauma
- History of trauma to ear
- Associated symptoms of ear infection
- History of viral illness, with/without use of salicylates
- History of ingestion of toxic substance, including alcohol (accidental or intentional, acute or chronic)
- History of previous CVA
- History of degenerative muscle disease such as multiple sclerosis, amyotrophic lateral sclerosis, etc
- Use of anticoagulant medications
- Symptoms of heat stroke

Objective

- Careful evaluation of vital signs; ensure that apparent ataxia is not orthostasis; particular attention to fever (may be associated with infectious encephalitis) or hyperthermic state

- If systemic process is suspected, evaluate respiratory status to ensure patient's ability to maintain airway and make adequate respiratory effort

- Neurologic evaluation with particular attention to asymmetric findings, limited extraocular movements, and/or obvious altered mental status

   Note: If patient is ambulatory, observe gait; ataxia and limp can be mistaken for one another

Assessment

- Symptoms of ataxia with evidence of:
   1. Metabolic derangement
   2. Toxic substance ingestion (specify)
   3. Developing neuromuscular sequelae
- Symptoms of ataxia with history of head trauma
- Symptoms of ataxia without obvious etiology

Plan

- Stat physician evaluation if symptoms are new
- Evaluate patient for mental status changes and respiratory status throughout stay in emergency department
- Do not allow patient to ambulate independently

Think

   1. Metabolic emergency (eg, Reye's syndrome)
   2. Guillain-Barré syndrome

3. Exacerbation of preexisting degenerative muscle disease
4. Ingestion or chronic use of toxic substance, particularly:
   - Dilantin
   - Sedatives
   - Alcohol (Wernicke-Korsakoff syndrome)
   - Glue
5. Heat stroke
6. Encephalitis, meningitis, other central nervous system infection
7. Intracranial lesion (CVA, mass)
8. Labyrinthitis (Meniere's syndrome)

CHANGE IN LEVEL OF CONSCIOUSNESS (ALTERED MENTAL STATUS)

Lisa Molitor

Subjective

- Onset and duration of symptoms (chronic state with progressive deterioration or acute)
- Character of alteration (depressed, agitated, confused, disoriented)
- History of alcohol use ("binge" or chronic)
- History of drug use:
  1. Depressed sensorium (depressants, opiates)
  2. Agitated sensorium (amphetamines, cocaine, etc)
- History of CVA, intracranial lesions, and/or metastatic disease
- Associated with trauma
- Evidence of dehydration/hypovolemia
- History of anticoagulant medications
- History of acute dyspnea
- History of chronic pulmonary disease

- History of metabolic disorders, such as diabetes, hypoglycemia, severe vomiting/diarrhea (puts patient at risk for electrolyte abnormalities and acid-base disturbances
- Recent viral syndrome with/without use of salicylates

Objective

- Patient's ability to maintain airway and breathe adequately
- Hemodynamic status
- General level of consciousness (Glasgow coma scale)
- Apparent type of status change (describe patient behavior: unresponsive, agitated, labile, confused, etc)
- Neurologic examination
- Evidence of anemia (assess heart rate, conjunctiva, nail beds, skin color)

Assessment

- Mental status change with apparent:
    1. Lethargy
    2. Agitation
    3. Confusion
    4. Disorientation
- Specify acute or progressive

Plan

- Depressed sensorium warrants immediate physician evaluation
- Agitation may be a sign of impending crisis; arrange expedited evaluation and monitor closely
- Acute mental status change warrants expedited physician evaluation
- Consider oxygen saturation measurement

Think

1. Hypoxemia induced
2. Shock induced
3. Hypoglycemia
4. Diabetic ketoacidosis
5. Reye's syndrome
6. Increased intracranial pressure
7. Wernicke-Korsakoff syndrome

Wernicke-Korsakoff syndrome is a complication of chronic alcohol use, occurring when thiamine stores are depleted. Physical findings include doubled vision, blurred vision, or becoming cross-eyed (nystagmus). Pupils are normal in size and reflexes are preserved. Staggering gait is a primary complaint in more than half the patients. There is mild to severe stance and gait ataxia. Abnormal mentation is present in more than 90% of patients. Signs/symptoms have a progressive onset over a period of days or weeks. Coma due to the syndrome manifests with miosis, absent doll's eyes, absent caloric reflexes, and depressed or absent DTRs. Mild hypothermia may be present. Hypotension may be present. The patient needs thiamine administered simultaneously with glucose.

BIBLIOGRAPHY

Harper C. Wernicke's encephalopathy: a more common disease than realized. *J Neurol*. 1979; 42.

Marx JA, Bar-Or D. Wernicke-Korsakoff syndrome. *Topics Emerg Med*. 1984; 6.

DIZZINESS/SYNCOPE ("PASSING OUT")

Lisa Molitor
Susan Somerson, ed.

Subjective

- Onset and duration of symptoms

- Activity engaged in when symptoms were experienced
- Accompanied by pain, nausea, hearing loss, visual disturbances, difficulty with ambulation
- History of middle ear disease or ear infection
- History of trauma, including lifting of heavy object
- History of hyperventilation
- History of cardiovascular disease and/or hypertension
- History of dysrhythmias, especially atrial fibrillation
- History of previous episodes
- History of diabetes or hypoglycemia
- History of anemia
- History of previous CVA or transient ischemic attack
- Possible ingestion of neurotoxic drugs and/or neurotoxic substances, including ethanol
- Concomitant palpitations, shortness of breath, chest pain
- History of heart problems, especially dysrhythmias and/or cardiovascular disease, or pacemaker
- Associated loss of vision
- Associated pain (facial, temporal, headache)
- Current medications (question carefully about dosage, recent change in dosage level, use of procholinergics by mouth or as eyedrops)
- Use of anticoagulant medications

Objective

- Observe ability to ambulate
- Neurologic (finger-to-nose test, holding palms steady in space, tandem gait, Romberg test)
- Optional fundoscopic examination, with special attention to evaluation for papilledema
- Pupil examination
- EOMs
- Gross hearing examination

- Evaluation of quality and regularity of pulse (if irregular, evaluate ECG rhythm)
- Orthostatic blood pressure
- Evaluation of respiratory status (rule out hypoxia and/or hyperventilation)

Assessment

- Presyncope
- Syncope
- Subjective weakness/dizziness with/without evidence of neurologic problems

Plan

- Stat physician evaluation if patient is cardiovascularly or hemodynamically unstable or obviously ataxic; if hypoxemia or toxic substance ingestion is suspected; if patient has tachycardia, bradycardia, irregular pulse with long pauses, or depressed sensorium; or if patient is hypotensive or hypertensive
- Initiate continuous ECG monitoring if warranted
- Consider oxygen saturation monitoring
- Do not allow patient to walk; use wheelchair or stretcher to transport (side rails up)

Think

1. Intracranial bleeding or lesion
2. Transient ischemic attack (prolonged confusion after a period of unconsciousness is suggestive of transient ischemic attack or seizure)[1]
3. Seizure
4. Labyrinthitis
5. Cardiovascular compromise with hypotension (consider acute myocardial infarction a possible cause)
6. Dehydration with hypotension

7. Dysrhythmias
8. Aortic stenosis
9. Pacemaker malfunction
10. Vasovagal episode, especially in elderly patients
11. Hypoxia and/or hyperventilation
12. Ingestion of toxic substance
13. Systemic:
    - Hypoglycemia
    - Hypoxia
    - Anemia
14. Allergic reaction resulting in vasodilation and hypotension
15. Drug hypersensitivity or overdose (drugs that are particularly likely to cause syncope include β blockers, digitalis preparations, quinidine, drugs with parasympathetic or procholinergic properties, antihypertensives, and antihistamines[1]

REFERENCE
1. Whiteside-Yim C. Syncope in the elderly: a clinical approach. *Geriatrics*. 1987;42:37-41.

NUMBNESS/TINGLING

Lisa Molitor

Subjective

- Onset and duration of symptoms
- Location of symptoms:
    1. Generalized
    2. Localized:
        —To face (specific site)
        —To extremities (one extremity or more than one)
- Accompanied by:
    1. Color change
    2. Respiratory distress, particularly tachypnea

  3. Loss of motor control (in face or extremities)
  4. Pain in proximal area
  5. Chest pain
- Associated with trauma to area
- History of:
  1. Long term alcohol use
  2. Diabetes mellitus
  3. Chronic anemia
  4. Recent viral syndrome
  5. Recent immunization
  6. Recent cat or dog bite or scratch
  7. Possible exposure to ticks

Objective

- Quantitate general level of distress
- If there is facial numbness, evaluate cranial nerves
- If there is facial numbness evaluate for motor sensory integrity in extremities
- If there is facial numbness evaluate level of consciousness
- Examine site for neurovascular integrity
- If extremity, carry out thorough examination
- Assess ability to ambulate, compare lower extremity function to upper extremity function (many progressive neurologic illnesses progress from distal to proximal), assess ability to stand from sitting position (if ambulatory)
- Optional: Elicit DTRs
- Concomitant respiratory distress related to neuromuscular symptoms (inability to expand chest)
- Assess for presence of fasciculations

Assessment

- Localized numbness/tingling of region (specify) with/ without history of trauma

- Numbness/tingling of regions (specify if more than one area involved) with/without history of trauma

Plan

- Expedite physician evaluation if:
  1. Evidence of respiratory compromise
  2. Accompanied by mental status changes
- Do not allow patient to ambulate independently

Think

1. Demyelinating disease such as Guillain-Barré syndrome, or myasthenia gravis resulting in poor chest excursion
2. Hyperventilation syndrome (determine why patient is hyperventilating)
3. CVA
4. Thromboembolus to peripheral structure
5. Nerve damage due to direct trauma or traumatic swelling
6. Lyme disease
7. Potential for falls: Do not allow patient to ambulate independently if at risk

SEIZURE

Lisa Molitor

Subjective

Subjective information may be best gathered from witnesses and/or caretakers

- First-time seizure or chronic disorder
- Time of seizure

- Duration of seizure activity and number of seizure episodes
- Description of seizure activity
- Report of trauma
- Report of vomiting
- Report of respiratory distress
- Concomitant loss of consciousness and/or incontinence
- Lucid interval
- Concomitant complaint of headache or other pain
- If first-time seizure:
    1. Precipitating events, including head trauma
    2. Ingestion of toxic substances, including drugs and alcohol
    3. Febrile illness
- If chronic seizure disorder:
    1. What is the preexisting neurologic abnormality?
    2. Is there a familial history of seizures?
    3. When was the last seizure before this episode?
    4. Is this usual seizure activity?
    5. Has patient taken medications as ordered?
    6. Does patient have clusters of seizures, and should another be expected?
    7. Do some things trigger seizures, such as stress?
    8. Does patient know when he or she is about to have a seizure? (If so, instruct patient to inform personnel in emergency department if aura occurs)

Objective

- Assessment of vital signs, with special emphasis on temperature and changes associated with Cushing's triad
- Neurologic assessment
- Respiratory assessment
- Signs/symptoms of hypoglycemia, especially in children
- Signs/symptoms of illicit drug use

- Examine tongue and oral structures for trauma

Assessment

- History of seizure activity associated with:
    1. Seizure disorder
    2. Head trauma
    3. Fever
    4. Ingestion of toxic substance
    5. Unknown cause

Plan

- Stat physician evaluation if:
    1. First-time seizure
    2. Hypoglycemia suspected
    3. Aspiration suspected and/or patient has signs of respiratory distress
    4. Head trauma suspected
    5. Seizure induced by cocaine or other toxic substance
    6. Increased intracranial pressure is suspected
- Anticipate some or all of the following physician orders:
    1. Supplemental oxygen
    2. Cardiac monitoring
    3. Stat evaluation of arterial blood gases, serum calcium, magnesium, standard electrolytes, glucose, Dilantin, phenobarbital, or other anticonvulsant serum levels (as indicated)
    4. Side rails up, with padding
    5. Keep vein open intravenous therapy
    6. Suction available at bedside

Think

1. Seizure associated with illicit drug use, particularly cocaine
2. Occult head trauma
3. Increased intracranial pressure
4. Meningitis/encephalitis

Section 8

Psychiatric/ Psychologic

8

PSYCHIATRIC/PSYCHOLOGIC SEQUELAE

Ramona Trebilcock
Lisa Molitor, ed.

Subjective

Note: Information gathering depends upon the patient's level of cooperation. If a patient presents in a belligerent, uncooperative state or was brought to the emergency department against his or her wishes, the triageur will need to be factual, firm, and in control of the situation. Avoid provoking the patient to greater anger or hostility.

- Determine patient's reason for visit; patient may make such statements as:
    1. I am hearing voices
    2. I am going crazy
    3. I need help
    4. I need to be admitted
    5. I feel like killing myself or someone else
    6. They are trying to kill me
    7. I can't stop crying
    8. Everyone is against me

- Make the following kinds of inquiries to assess patients in behavioral crisis:

  1. Are drugs and/or alcohol involved?
  2. Have you ever had a problem like this before or felt this way before?
  3. Have you seen anyone about this problem?
  4. Do you have a psychiatrist?
  5. Is anyone with you? Do you have a support person or system?
  6. Do you hurt anywhere? Are you having any pain?
  7. Are you hearing voices or seeing things? If so, what do the voices say to you? What are you seeing?
  8. Are you having problems eating? (poor dietary intake can produce behavior changes)
  9. Are you having problems sleeping?
  10. Are you taking any medications or using alcohol or street drugs? When was the last time you took any of these?
  11. Are you having thoughts of hurting yourself or someone else? Do you feel out of control now?
  12. Do you know where you are now?
  13. Do you have a history of headaches or head trauma?

Note: Do not attempt to touch the patient if he or she is agitated.

Objective

- Level of consciousness and orientation
- Evidence of trauma to head or other body parts
- Observe for agitation (pacing suggests agitation)
- Note inflection in voice (angry, hostile, quiet, silent)
- Affect (flat, loud, subdued)
- Eye contact
- Level of cooperation
- General appearance
- Conversational engagement (flight of ideas, word salad, refusing to answer)
- Hallucinations

- Skin (appearance, temperature, presence of needle marks)

Assessment

- Behavior change (specify type) with apparent psychiatric/psychologic etiology

Plan

- Immediate/critical
    1. Expressing suicidal ideation, feeling out of control
    2. Extreme agitation; is threatening, demanding, shouting; has weapon
    3. Expresses desire to harm someone else
- Emergent
    1. Expressing suicidal ideation but not out of control
    2. Hallucinating but able to maintain self in public
    3. Intoxicated without respiratory or physical compromise
    4. Depressed but not agitated or at risk for elopement
    5. Anxious
- Delayed
    1. Medication refills
    2. Scheduled for admission to open psychiatric unit

The patient may require restraint upon arrival to the emergency department. Assure the patient that you are there to help. Be sure there is sufficient staff and security personnel available before attempting to restrain the patient. If the patient has a weapon, immediately clear personnel and other patients from the area and notify security personnel and police. See Table 8-1.

Think

1. *Psychotic:* Hallucinating, violent, out of control (restrain)

Table 8–1 Quick Reference to Identification of Behavioral Sequelae.

	Anxiety	Agitation	Sadness	Combative	Verbal	Nonverbal	Guilt	Anger	Hallucinations	Pain	Crying	Stoic	Positive Eye Contact	Cooperative	Flat Affect	Altered Thought Process	Violent	Potential to Injure Self or Others	Decreased LOC	Requires Restraints	Argumentative
Psychotic		✓		✓	✓			✓	✓				✓			✓	✓	✓		✓	✓
Depressed			✓			✓	✓				✓	✓		✓	✓			✓			
Suicidal		✓				✓	✓		✓			✓			✓	✓		✓		✓	
Physical Abuse	✓		✓			✓	✓	✓		✓	✓	✓		✓	✓						
Sexual Abuse	✓		✓	✓	✓	✓	✓	✓		✓		✓		✓	✓						✓
Drug Intoxication	✓	✓		✓	✓			✓	✓		✓					✓	✓	✓	✓	✓	✓
Alcohol Intoxication		✓		✓	✓			✓	✓							✓	✓	✓	✓	✓	
Frightened		✓		✓	✓			✓		✓	✓	✓	✓	✓			✓				
Grieving	✓		✓	✓	✓		✓	✓		✓	✓	✓	✓		✓						✓
Headaches—Head Trauma	✓	✓		✓	✓			✓	✓	✓						✓	✓	✓	✓	✓	✓
Diseases		✓			✓				✓	✓					✓	✓	✓	✓	✓	✓	
Anxiety	✓	✓									✓		✓	✓				✓			
Borderline								✓					✓			✓					✓

2. *Drug-induced behavior:* May require restraints
3. *Depression:* May be due to drugs, death in family, divorce, holiday, anniversary, loneliness
4. *Head injury:* Can produce behavior changes that may mimic psychotic behavior
5. *Headache:* When behavior changes accompany headache, consider intracranial lesion as cause
6. *Systemic disease:* Tertiary syphilis, alcoholism, Creutzfeldt-Jakob disease
7. *Inhalation injuries:* Smoke or chemical inhalation may produce behavior changes
8. *Abuse:* "Acting out" may be a response to physical/ sexual abuse
9. *Alzheimer's disease/dementia:* Suspect based on progressive history

GUIDELINES FOR SPECIFIC SITUATIONS

In any behavioral emergency, the most important thing you can do is "be there." This means be available, caring, understanding, and physically present and providing a sense that this situation is the most important thing you have to deal with at the time. Fear of patients, especially psychotic patients, will be sensed. Laughing or joking may be perceived as antagonistic or as directed toward the patient. With all behavioral emergencies, time is essential, and the amount of time spent with the patient is important. It will take time to have these patients express themselves, and it may be helpful to ask pertinent questions at triage to gain information and then have another staff member talk in depth with the patient elsewhere in the emergency department.

Do not argue with the patient. You can only lose. This is most important when dealing with those under the influence of inebriating substances and those with antisocial and borderline personalities.

Hostile, agitated patients need gentle control, which means you must be in control. You may let the patient know it is not acceptable to behave in abusive or destructive ways (eg, throwing things) in your "house." Sometimes this statement helps. You may also want to give them behavior restriction. Do not lie to the patient.

Abuse

Physical abuse at any age is traumatic. The patient may be nonverbal and in shock, angry, crying, or out of control. It is most helpful if you can get the patient to express his or her feelings verbally about the situation. Behavior may be the only means of communication about the feelings that are being experienced, however. Children who have been abused are usually quiet, passive, and nonverbal. They will observe all adults, perhaps warily. Children who have been abused less frequently may withdraw when approached. Children with a long history of abuse will watch adults with "seared" eyes and may not withdraw or even cry when pinched, sutured, or given an injection.

Behavioral Crisis

Severe agitation, depression, and anxiety are best dealt with in a calm, factual, and understanding manner. Reassure the patient that you realize he or she is in emotional pain and that you will try to help. Take care to observe patients who are severely depressed. They are at greatest risk for suicide and may not verbalize their feelings or plans.

Delusions

Delusions can be dealt with in the same manner as hallucinations. If the patient is afraid that he or she is being followed or that someone is coming to kill him or her, take the patient inside the emergency department and reassure him or her that you will help. This will prevent panic by the patient and by other patients and visitors in the waiting area. Ensure that the patient is not provoked or encouraged by others.

Fear and Grieving

Your presence, caring, and concern are the most significant interventions for fear and grieving. Most of the time, touch is helpful for the grieving individual.

Life-Threatening Situations

Life-threatening conditions in the self or a loved one usually provoke anger. Family members will be demanding and hostile. The self and family are reacting out of fear. If you can identify with the fear, patients are likely to be more verbal with you.

Sexual Abuse

Refer to the section above. Teen or adult females may feel dirty and become obsessed with trying to get themselves clean. Males who have been sexually abused may react with less emotion but often require more opportunity to verbalize. Children experience guilt associated with imagining that they have done something wrong to have caused the abuse to occur.

Hallucinations

Patients presenting with hallucinations can be approached factually in an effort to gather information. If the patient becomes lost in a hallucination, you can attempt to bring him or her back by asking questions about medications, how long he or she has seen or thought this, and so forth. If the patient presses you to participate in a hallucination, you can introduce reasonable doubt (ie, "You may see that, but I do not"). Do not tell the patient that he or she is crazy or stupid. Be factual and professional.

Section 9

Respiratory

COUGH/COUGHING

Lisa Molitor
Paula Turvy McCarty, ed.

Subjective

- Onset/duration of symptoms
- Character of cough:
    1. Dry
    2. Productive (characterize sputum: color, consistency, amount, blood-tinged)
- If acute:
    1. Associated with wheezing and/or shortness of breath
    2. Associated with foreign body aspiration
- If chronic:
    1. Associated with fever
    2. Change in sputum color
    3. Weight loss
    4. History of tuberculosis
- History of:
    1. Pulmonary disease

2. Cardiac disease
- Medications in use, particularly captropril

Objective

- Presence and degree of respiratory distress
- Auscultate breath sounds
- Febrile, tachypneic, tachycardic

Assessment

- Acute or chronic onset of cough
- Cough with/without evidence of infectious process
- Cough with/without evidence of respiratory distress

Plan

- Stat physician evaluation if:
    1. Foreign body aspiration is suspected
    2. Respiratory distress present, patient is tachypneic
    3. Evidence of pulmonary edema/cardiac asthma present
    4. Patient is tachycardic
- Expedite physician evaluation if:
    1. Patient is febrile
    2. Condition appears toxic
- Institute respiratory isolation if:
    1. Cough is productive of large amount of sputum or sputum is bloody
    2. Tuberculosis or other infectious respiratory disease is suspected
- Avoid patient contact with others who may be immunocompromised and pediatric patients

Think

1. Foreign body aspiration, particularly in children, elderly or impaired patients, intoxicated patients

2. Cardiac asthma

3. Infectious disease (institute isolation per protocol)

DYSPNEA/SHORTNESS OF BREATH/ RESPIRATORY DISTRESS

Paula Turvy McCarty
Lisa Molitor, ed.

Subjective

- Onset and duration of signs/symptoms
- Patient's description of level of comfort
- Patient's description of presence and severity of orthopnea
- Any precipitating factors:
  1. Where it started
  2. When it started
  3. Exercise
  4. Presence of anxiety before onset
  5. Exposure to toxins, allergens, chemicals, irritants
  6. Presence of stressful events at time of onset
- Associated conditions:
  1. Trauma to neck, mouth, upper chest
  2. Presence of respiratory infection
  3. History of cardiac conditions and/or chest pain
  4. History of other episodes
  5. Recent confinement to bed or similar decrease in level of activity
  6. Recent long bone fracture or surgery
- Medication history
- History of allergies
- Precipitating, alleviating, and/or worsening factors
- Medical history:
  1. Asthma or reactive airway disease
  2. Cardiac conditions
  3. Respiratory infections

4. Chronic lung disease
5. Clotting disorders, particularly thrombus formation
- Nocturnal dyspnea
- Presence of angina equivalents (diaphoresis, shortness of breath, indigestion, sensation of pressure without actual pain)
- Recent unexplained weight loss
- Smoker (pack/year history)
- Use of oral contraceptives

Objective

- Patient's ability to speak comfortably, ability to answer questions with full sentences rather than short, labored responses (history may best be provided by bystanders or caregivers)
- Appearance
  1. Skin color, especially around lips, nail beds, conjunctivae
  2. Respiratory rate, presence of tachypnea or bradypnea
  3. Chest wall movement, symmetry and depth of expansion
  4. Presence of diaphoresis
  5. If sequelae are long term, assess for dehydration
  6. Skin temperature (assess peripheral and central structures)
  7. Psychologic status (presence of anxiety, agitation, sense of impending doom)
  8. Use of accessory breathing muscles
- Audibility of breathing (assess without stethoscope):
  1. Audible wheezing
  2. Audible stridor
  3. Snoring sounds
- Assessment of cough (dry, productive, "wet")
- Rate, quality, depth of respirations (assess for full 60 seconds)

- Auscultation of breath sounds
  1. Type of sound (normal or adventitious; see "Wheezing")
  2. Presence of rales (do not clear with cough)
  3. Presence of rhonchi (may improve or clear with cough; rales and rhonchi may be charted as crackles)
  4. Presence of pleural friction rub
  5. Presence of decreased or distant sounds (when comparing sounds heard in various areas of chest)
  6. Absence of sounds (usually indicates urgent situation)
  7. Relative equality of sounds heard during systematic auscultation
  8. Degree of air exchange
- Palpation of chest:
  1. Bilateral, abnormal chest wall movement
  2. Presence of crepitus
  3. Pain elicited by palpation
- Patient posture and carriage:
  1. Upright posture
  2. Barrel chested
  3. Unable to lie flat or with head of bed below 45°
- Specific vital sign changes:
  1. Dyspnea and shortness of breath usually produce tachycardia
  2. Tachypnea is an early sign of respiratory distress and hypoxia
  3. Bradypnea may suggest sequelae involving neurologic system (bradypnea is usually a late sign of hypoxia; Kussmaul's pattern is associated with diabetic ketoacidosis; Cheyne-Stokes pattern associated with neurologic sequelae)
- Blood pressure assessment including assessment for pulsus paradoxus
- Temperature assessment (oral readings may be decreased by mouth breathing)
- Oxygen saturation measurement

Assessment

- Dyspnea/shortness of breath with signs/symptoms of:
  1. Pneumothorax
  2. Congestive heart failure
  3. Hyperventilation syndrome
  4. Chest pain
  5. Reactive airway disease/asthma
  6. Hemothorax
  7. Pleural effusion
  8. History of trauma
  9. Evidence of concomitant neurologic sequelae
  10. Infectious process

- Respiratory failure (oxygenation and/or ventilation are inadequate to sustain life)

- Subjective shortness of breath without objective findings

Plan

- Reassurance

- Institute oxygen saturation monitoring

- Stat physician evaluation if actual and/or impending respiratory decompensation is suspected

- Continuous observation of patients who are seriously ill

- Anticipate some or all of the following physician orders as judged from specific situation:
  1. Chest x-ray examination
  2. Arterial blood gas sampling
  3. Supplemental oxygen
  4. Cardiac monitoring (bedside monitoring and/or telemetry)
  5. Continuous oxygenation saturation monitoring
  6. Peak flow measurement (may be assessed in triage area)
  7. Medications as needed
  8. Invasive procedures as needed

- Respiratory isolation if infectious process suspected

Think

1. Chronic use of salicylates or acute ingestion leading to induced metabolic acidosis and associated tachypnea
2. Stasis emboli
3. Fat embolism
4. Pneumothorax
5. Congestive heart failure
6. Hyperventilation syndrome (determine why patient is hyperventilating)
7. Chest pain may herald pulmonary embolism or cardiac event
8. Reactive airway disease/asthma
9. Hemothorax
10. Pleural effusion
11. History of trauma
12. Evidence of concomitant neurologic sequelae
13. Infectious process
14. Pulmonary embolism
15. Altitude sickness (with associated pulmonary edema)

WHEEZING

Paula Turvy McCarty
Lisa Molitor, ed.

Subjective

- Chief complaint, including duration of symptoms
- Previous history of wheezing and/or diagnosed asthma
- Precipitating factors:
  1. Asthma by history
  2. Weather change
  3. Exposure to toxins or air pollutants
  4. History of chronic obstructive pulmonary disease
  5. Current illnesses or infections, especially upper respiratory infection symptoms

6. Food allergies, plant allergies, "hay fever"
7. Exposure to known allergic antigens, history of known allergy
8. New medications
9. New foods
10. Ingestion of salicylates (aspirin-induced asthma)
11. Exercise
12. Emotional factors
13. Irritants (dust, chemicals)
14. Insect bite

- Self-treatment attempted and results, including self-medication
- History of cardiac disease
- Use of β-blocking agents, especially Lopressor or Inderal
- Recent unexplained weight loss

Objective

- General level of comfort, including ability to speak in complete sentences rather than in halting speech pattern
- Presence of audible wheezes
- Skin color, temperature
- Nail bed color/conjunctivae color
- Presence of diaphoresis
- Careful assessment of respiratory status:

  1. Respiratory rate, effort, inspiration-expiration volume ratio
  2. Nasal flaring, chest retractions, prolonged expiration
  3. Use of accessory muscles
  4. Presence and character of cough (note color of sputum if present)
  5. Presence of concomitant central nervous system signs (increased anxiety/agitation, lethargy, dilated or constricted pupils, trembling)
  6. Quality of air exchange

Assessment

- Wheezing which is:
    1. Audible without stethoscope
    2. Audible on auscultation with stethoscope
    3. In known asthmatic or COPD patient for first time
    4. With history of allergen, chemical, or drug exposure
    5. With physical findings suggestive of cardiac asthma

Plan

- Reassure patient, obtain immediate physician evaluation
- Initiate airway management procedures, as needed
- Position patient in Fowler's position
- Initiate cardiac monitoring
- Initiate oxygen saturation measurement
- Anticipate some or all of the following physician orders:
    1. Oxygen
    2. Peak flow spirometry
    3. Arterial blood gas measurement
    4. Nebulizer treatment
    5. Bronchodilator
    6. Intravenous hydration, if indicated
    7. Laboratory measurement of theophylline level, complete blood count with differential, electrolytes as situation warrants
    8. Continuous oxygen saturation monitoring

Think

1. Stage I status asthmaticus:
    - Nasal flaring, chest retractions, prolonged expirations
    - Tachycardia, tachypnea
2. Stage II status asthmaticus:
    - Nasal flaring, use of accessory neck muscles
    - Decreased ability to cough
    - Cyanosis

- Positive pulsus paradoxus
- Retention of carbon dioxide, increased heart rate, pupillary constriction
- Subjective feeling of warmth

3. Stage III status asthmaticus:

- Decreased wheezing, "silent chest"
- Minimal movement of chest secondary to exhaustion, resulting in decreased gas exchange
- Central nervous system changes, including drowsiness, muscle twitching
- Increased carbon dioxide tension (> 70 mm Hg can produce seizures, coma)

4. Tachypnea suggests early respiratory failure, bradypnea suggests late respiratory failure[1]

REFERENCE

1. Ronshausen CA. A respiratory emergency. In: Parker JG, ed. *Emergency Nursing: A Guide to Comprehensive Care*. New York: Wiley; 1984.

Section 10

Trauma

BURNS

Lisa Molitor
Mary Beasley, ed.

Subjective

- Time of injury
- Circumstances of injury
- Source of burn/mechanism of injury (thermal, electrical [if electrical, see below], chemical, radiation, scalding, contact with hot surface)
- Smoke or toxic fume inhalation (patient was in enclosed space)
- Other trauma unnoticed by patient secondary to severe pain, anxiety, etc
- Exposure of eyes to high heat, chemicals, radiation, bright light
- Self-treatment attempted
- Treatment applied by other health professionals before arrival
- General state of patient's health, particularly history of alcohol or drug use, history of pulmonary and/or cardiac disease.

- Last tetanus toxoid (other immunizations up to date)
- History of smoking, chronic obstructive pulmonary disease, or other chronic respiratory diseases

Objective

- General level of distress
- Hemodynamic status
- If smoke inhalation is possible and/or if burns are around upper body, face, or head, evaluate respiratory status
- Description of wound (location, approximate size, color, presence of exudate and/or bleeding, odor present if any, presence of contaminating debris)
- If burn to extremity, determine whether it is circumferential (if so, evaluate extremity perfusion with Doppler)
- If burn to chest area, determine whether it is circumferential (chest excursion affected)
- Estimate degree, if possible (see below)
- Estimate percentage of body area burned (general guide: surface area of hand roughly equals 1% of body surface area; see Fig. 10-1)

Assessment

- Status postburn (specify type: thermal, chemical, etc; specify localized body part and percentage of body surface affected)
- Status postburn with/without evidence of smoke inhalation injury

Plan

- Immediate physician evaluation if respiratory or hemodynamic compromise present

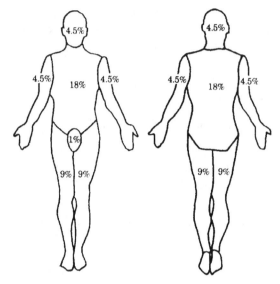

Figure 10–1 Rule of Nines. *Source*: Reprinted from *Manual of Burn Therapeutics: An Interdisciplinary Approach* by R.E. Salisbury, NM Newman, and G.P. Dingeldein, p. 13, with permission of Little, Brown & Company, © 1983.

- Immediate physician evaluation if greater than 10% of body surface area is affected

- Immediate physician evaluation if circumferential burn to extremity

- Immediate physician evaluation if electrical burn and institute electrocardiographic monitoring

- Immediate evaluation if burn has chemical source

- Immediate evaluation if eyes are affected

- Immediate evaluation if child

Think

1. Predisposing factors suggesting a need for airway evaluation:

   - Closed space injury
   - Burns to face, neck

- Presence of singed nasal hairs, eyebrows, eyelashes
- Complaints of hoarseness, sore throat, tightness in throat/chest
- Shortness of breath, dyspnea, tachypnea, reddened pharynx, soot in oral cavity
- Increasing facial/neck edema

2. Anticipate development of respiratory distress if inhalation is possible
3. Evaluate hemodynamic status carefully and monitor diligently if patient is fluid resuscitated
4. Anticipate that patient cooperation will be poor if pain is severe (early pain control is helpful)
5. If patient is a child, elderly, or incapacitated, consider possibility of abuse as cause

GUIDELINES TO ESTIMATING RELATIVE BURN SEVERITY

- Degree ratings of burns:
    1. Partial thickness (pink, wet, blanches with pressure, blisters present)
    2. Full thickness (discolored [white, brown, black], leathery consistency, dry)
    3. Complete or fourth degree (muscle, bone injury observed)
- Factors determining extent of injury in electrical burns:
    1. Type of current (AC or DC)
    2. Voltage
    3. Resistance
    4. Resistance of tissues involved
    5. Pathway of current
    6. Duration of contact
- Relative resistance of body tissues to current flow:

High—Bone–Fat–Tendon–Skin–Muscle–Blood–Nerve—**Low**

Because of the high electrical resistance of bone, excessive heat is produced when current is conducted through it. Deep structures surrounding the bone may be injured while more superficial structures remain viable. Therefore, the severity of the injury may not be apparent upon examination soon after the injury.[1]

REFERENCE

1. McDougal J. *Manual of Burns*. New York: Springer-Verlag; 1978.

EXTREMITY TRAUMA/EXTREMITY PAIN

Lisa Molitor

Subjective

- Onset and duration of symptoms
- Location of pain
- Description of pain
- Pain constant or intermittent (if intermittent, onset related to a particular activity, including rest)
- Pain related to trauma
- Statement of general health
- History of clotting disorders
- Concomitant chest pain, shortness of breath, or other symptoms of pulmonary embolism
- History of Raynaud's phenomenon or peripheral vascular disease

Objective

- Relative degree of distress
- Compare affected extremity to contralateral extremity and document:
  1. Obvious deformity
  2. Tenderness
  3. Skin temperature

4. Capillary refill time
5. Swelling
6. Discoloration, including erythema, ecchymosis
7. Breaks in skin
8. Edema (pitting or non-pitting)
9. Palpable crepitus

- Neurovascular examination
- Specific examinations:
    1. Fingers:
        —Metacarpal/phalangeal tenderness
        —Integrity of collateral ligaments
        —Range of motion
        —Flexion and extension
        —Optional: two-point discrimination
    2. Hand:
        —Metacarpal/phalangeal tenderness
    3. Wrist:
        —Metacarpal/phalangeal tenderness
        —Navicular tenderness
    4. Forearm:
        —Pronation and supination
    5. Elbow:
        —Range of motion including pronation and supination
    6. Toes:
        —Capillary refill—quantitate time
    7. Foot:
        —Metatarsal/phalangeal tenderness
        —Palpate base of fifth metatarsal
        —Palpate pedal pulses (posterior tibial and femoral)
    8. Ankle:
        —Range of motion
    9. Lower leg:
        —Palpable tenderness
        —Presence/absence of Homans' sign

- If thrombus/embolism suspected, conduct pulmonary examination

Assessment

- Painful (identify extremity involved) with/without history of trauma

Plan

- Stop any bleeding with sterile dressing and elevation of affected part; if bleeding is severe, apply pressure to supplemental artery
- Splint according to injury in position of function as per unit protocol
- Apply ice to area as per unit protocol
- If deformity exists, "splint it as it lies"
- If neurovascular and/or sensory deficit is present, obtain immediate physician evaluation

Think

1. Occult fracture, especially in children or the elderly
2. Potential for soft tissue injury in unsplinted fractures
3. Ischemia related to:
   - Thrombus
   - Peripheral vascular disease
   - Traumatic interruption in blood supply
   - Compartment syndrome

EYE TRAUMA

Lisa Molitor

See also "Eye Pain"

Subjective

- Time of insult
- Mechanism of injury and circumstances
- Associated pain, tearing, redness
- Any treatment by self or health care providers
- Current medications
- Sensation of foreign body
- Use of contact lenses
- Exposure to high heat, chemicals, or radiation

Objective

- General level of distress
- Gross measurement of visual acuity (Snellen's chart at 20 ft)
- Documentation of appearance of anterior chamber, pupil response, periorbital swelling, loss of skin integrity
- Documentation of EOMs if associated with trauma (rule out nerve entrapment)
- Associated discharge, injected appearance

Assessment

- Type of ocular trauma (specify type):
    1. Eyelid laceration
    2. Foreign body injuries, penetration possible:
       —Superficial
       —Involving corneal abrasion
       —Dislocated contact lens
       —Corneal laceration/penetrating injury
    3. Blunt injury to eye
    4. Radiation injury
    5. Ocular burns:

—Thermal

—Chemical

Plan

- Irrigate eye as indicated per unit protocol
- Expedite physician evaluation
- Elevate head of bed 30° with supine positioning

Think

1. Acute glaucoma
2. Retinal detachment
3. Penetrating foreign body

LACERATIONS

Lisa Molitor

Subjective

- Time of injury
- Mechanism of injury (occult injuries to other body parts)
- Mechanism of injury associated with contaminated object or surface
- Date of last tetanus toxoid
- Report of contaminating substances in wound
- Sensation of foreign body in wound
- Self-treatment attempted (specify)

Objective

- Evaluation of hemodynamic status if wound is severe or if there is significant history of trauma

- Location of wound
- Estimated size of wound (length and depth)
- Shape of wound (linear, jagged, stellate, puncture)
- Document presence or absence of amputation or avulsion
- If wound to an extremity:
  1. Gross neurologic examination
  2. Evaluation of blood supply to areas distal to wound
  3. Bleeding status (not actively bleeding, oozing, clot present, actively bleeding, pulsatile bleeding)

Assessment

- Laceration to affected part (name) with/without evidence of neurovascular compromise
- Document size of wound, in centimeters
- Document presence or absence of active bleeding

Plan

- Stop any bleeding with direct pressure via sterile dressing, elevation of affected part, pressure on supplemental artery if needed
- Splint area as indicated
- Arrange immediate evaluation of wound per physician as severity indicates
- Anticipate some or all of the following physician orders:
  1. Tetanus toxoid administration
  2. Irrigation of wound
  3. Radiographs of affected area
  4. Preparation for repair in emergency department or operating room, as required
  5. If significant bleeding has occurred, complete blood count, frequent vital signs, infusion of intravenous fluids

Think

1. Hemodynamic instability secondary to blood loss
2. Arterial injury if bleeding is pulsatile

MULTISYSTEM TRAUMA

Lisa Molitor

Note: Assessment and Plan for this section should be based on individual department protocol.

Primary Survey

- Assess airway
- Assess breathing and circulation
- Stop any bleeding
- Assess for shock

Secondary Survey

- Brief neurologic examination:
    1. Level of consciousness
        - *A* Alert
        - *V* Responds to verbal stimuli
        - *P* Responds to pain
        - *U* Unresponsive
    2. Motor (movement of fingers and toes to command)
    3. Sensation (assess distal to proximal)
    4. Pupils:
        - Equal
        - Round
        - React to light
        - Accommodate
- Abdominal examination:

1. Inspect
2. Auscultate
3. Palpate

- Assess and splint extremity fractures
- Assess neurovascular status before and after splinting
- Maxillofacial trauma:
    1. Assume cervical spine injury
    2. Suspect head injury
    3. Constantly monitor airway

Subjective

Note: In many if not most situations, subjective information is best gathered from rescue personnel.

- Estimated time of trauma
- Mechanism of injuries
- Hemodynamic, respiratory, and neurologic status before arrival at hospital
- Location of apparent injuries
- Resuscitation interventions applied at scene and en route
- Known use of alcohol and/or drugs before traumatic incident
- General state of patient's health, if known, including any preexisting medical problems

Trauma to Specific Regions

Abdominal Trauma

- Subjective
    1. Mechanism of injury (penetrating: stab wound, missile, spattering projectiles; nonpenetrating:blunt object, seat belt, crushing injury)
    2. History of previous surgery

- Objective
  1. *Inspection*: Look for breaks in skin, bruising, abrasions, discoloration, Grey Turner's sign (bruising around flanks, suggestive of retroperitoneal hematoma), old surgical scars
  2. *Auscultation*: (systematic auscultation in all four quadrants for at least 1 minute) bowel sounds, abdominal bruit
  3. *Palpation*: (may be deferred to physician's examination) Start in area remote from site of pain, assess for increased pain with local palpation, involuntary guarding, palpable enlargement of peritoneal organ or mass, rebound tenderness

Chest Trauma

- Evaluate for presence of Hamman's crunch
- See "Dyspnea/Shortness of Breath"

Head Trauma

- Subjective
  1. Mechanism of injury
  2. Loss of consciousness (duration)
  3. Seizure activity
  4. Memory of events surrounding incident
  5. Patient's ability to identify present surroundings and personnel
- Objective
  1. Glasgow coma scale
  2. Level of orientation:

  —Person

  —Place

  —Time

  —Events

  3. Respiratory status
  4. Description of wounds, bleeding, etc
  5. Document presence/absence of Battle's sign, raccoon eyes

Pelvic Trauma

- Subjective
    1. Mechanism of injury
    2. Estimated time of last urination
    3. Last intake of food/drink
    4. In women, possibility of pregnancy; menstruating
    5. Other sites of pain

- Objective
    1. Examine perineum for lacerations, ecchymosis, swelling, obvious deformity, bleeding (from urethra, rectum, vagina)
    2. Palpate symphysis pubis and iliac wings to assess relative pelvic stability.

- Plan
    1. Do not insert urinary catheter without direct physician order, probably after urethrocystogram has been obtained
    2. Monitor urine output carefully and test urine for blood

BIBLIOGRAPHY

Orban DJ, Molitor L. Abdominal trauma. In: Cahill & Balskus. *Intervention in Emergency Nursing.* Gaithersburg, Md.: Aspen; 1986:203-224.

NEAR DROWNING

Lisa Molitor

Subjective

- Approximate time of incident
- Circumstances surrounding incident
- Salt water or fresh water
- Approximate time of submersion

- Air/water temperature, if known
- Resuscitation efforts by bystanders and rescue personnel
- Other injuries sustained, especially diving injuries with head and/or cervical spine trauma
- State of health previous to incident
- History of smoking, chronic obstructive pulmonary disease, or other respiratory illnesses that may make artificial ventilation difficult

Objective

- Standard evaluation of vital signs
- Evaluation of respiratory status
- Appearance (skin color, especially around lips, nail beds, conjunctivae)
- If breathing spontaneously:
    1. Respiratory rate, presence of tachypnea or bradypnea
    2. Chest wall movement, symmetry and depth of expansion
    3. Rate, quality, and depth of respirations (assess for full 60 seconds)
- Auscultation of breath sounds
    1. Type of sound (normal or adventitious; see "Wheezing")
    2. Presence of rales (do not clear with cough or suctioning)
    3. Presence of rhonchi (may improve or clear with cough or suctioning; rales and rhonchi may be charted as "crackles")
    4. Presence of pleural friction rub
    5. Presence of decreased or distant sounds (when comparing sounds heard in various areas of chest)
    6. Absence of sounds (indicates urgent situation)
    7. Relative equality of sounds heard during systematic auscultation

- Evaluation of level of consciousness (orientation to person, place, time, and events; see Glasgow coma scale assessment)

Assessment

- Status post–near drowning in:
  1. Salt water
  2. Fresh water
- Status post–near drowning with/without evidence of:
  1. Respiratory compromise
  2. Neurologic sequelae

Plan

- Stat physician evaluation
- Maintain airway, ventilation, and circulation as needed
- In addition to basic ABC (airway, breathing, circulation) interventions, anticipate some or all of the following physician orders:
  1. Chest x-ray examination
  2. Intravenous line established and maintained
  3. Arterial blood gas sampling
  4. 12-Lead ECG
  5. Measurement of rectal/core temperature upon arrival and frequently thereafter
  6. Standard laboratory serum studies
  7. Admission to hospital (probable intensive care unit admission)
  8. If diving injury, cervical spine immobilization, cervical spine x-ray evaluation
  9. Continuous oxygen saturation monitoring

Think

1. *Patient who has sustained near-drowning trauma may decompensate acutely after a relatively stable*

period immediately after the incident, especially in cases of salt water aspiration
2. Assume that cervical spine injury and possible head trauma has occurred until physician evaluation clears the patient's status

Part II

Pediatric Emergency Triage

Section 11

Pediatric

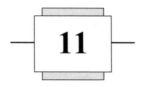

ASSESSMENT GUIDELINES

In assessing children, many of the same guidelines covered in other sections of this book apply. The presentation of certain problems, however, can be markedly different in the pediatric population. The following is an abbreviated list of critical signs/symptoms that may signal a true emergency in children.

- Cardiovascular
    1. Decreased peripheral pulses and/or slow capillary refill time
    2. Tachycardia not associated with crying or agitation (Table 11-1)
    3. Hypotension
    4. Bradycardia
- Gastrointestinal
    1. Gastrointestinal bleeding
    2. Frequent vomiting
    3. Abdominal pain
    4. Diarrhea
    5. Abdominal distension
- Genitourinary
    1. Status post straddle injury
    2. Painful testes or scrotum

Table 11-1 Relative Tachycardia in Children

Age (years)	Heart Rate (beat/min): Upper Limit of Normal Range
< 1	200
1–2	160
2–6	120
6–10	110
>10	100

Note: Children are often frightened in the emergency department, and catecholamine release has a direct effect on heart rate. It is important to reassess heart rate during the child's stay, especially as the child calms.

Source: Adapted from *Basic Trauma Life Support* by J Campbell, Prentice Hall, © 1985

---

 3. Vaginal bleeding

 4. Hematuria

 5. Penile or vaginal trauma

- General findings

 1. Trauma

 2. Fever

 3. Lethargy or irritability

 4. Apparent dehydration

 5. Poisoning

 6. Cyanosis and/or respiratory distress

 7. Change in mentation

 8. Drowning/near drowning

 9. Burns

 10. Suspected child abuse and/or rape

- Head, ears, eyes, nose, throat

 1. Stiff neck

 2. Facial cellulitis

 3. Periorbital cellulitis

 4. Drooling

 5. Sore throat/difficulty swallowing

 6. Severe epistaxis

- Musculoskeletal

 1. Arthritis

 2. Bone pain

 3. Torticollis

    4. Limp

    5. Refusal to use extremity

- Neurologic

    1. Any unexplained change in mental status

    2. Seizures

    3. Ataxia

    4. Dizziness/syncope

    5. Asymmetry of neurologic findings

    6. Headache

- Respiratory

    1. Stridor/wheezing

    2. Retractions

    3. Dyspnea

    4. Cough

    5. History of "turning blue" or apnea

    6. Chest pain

    7. Tachypnea not associated with agitation

    8. History of foreign body aspiration

- Skin

    1. Petechiae, purpura

    2. Exfoliative dermatitis

    3. Urticaria

    4. Lacerations

    5. Cyanosis or mottled skin

COMMON PRESENTING COMPLAINTS

Some of the more common presenting complaints involving pediatric patients are covered in this section. The reader is encouraged to refer to the major sections covering these topics in the text. In assessing children, however, the following guidelines may be particularly useful.

Cellulitis

Cellulitis in children can produce sepsis quickly. Thorough hemodynamic evaluation of a sick child with an apparent cellulitis is in order. Periorbital cellulitis can produce severe complications in children and warrants admission in most institutions. A child with periorbital cellulitis should be evaluated by a physician expediently.

Dehydration

Dehydration is a potentially life-threatening state. The following list of subjective and objective findings will help determine the degree of dehydration:

- Subjective
    1. Concomitant symptoms such as vomiting, diarrhea, poor intake of fluids, fever
    2. Failure to urinate for more than 6 hours (can be difficult to assess if child is having frequent diarrhea); quantitate urine output as much as possible (number of wet diapers, etc)
- Objective
    1. Tearless cry
    2. Dry oral mucosa
    3. Sunken fontanelle(s)
    4. Poor skin turgor
    5. Irritability/lethargy

Warning signs of serious dehydration: serum sodium greater than 150 mg/dL, hematuria, urine output less than 1 mL/kg/hour after fluid resuscitation of 20 mL/kg IVP is administered

Diarrhea

Diarrhea is a common presenting complaint in the pediatric population. Its causes are often relatively benign, but diarrhea can produce dehydration and electrolyte disturbances, including acidosis, precipitously in infants and small children. In benign cases, the emergency department management is aimed at recognizing, treating, and/ or preventing dehydration, and treating the cause of the diarrhea if it is infectious.

There are a few possible serious causes of diarrhea worth considering in the triage area:

• Sepsis
• Appendicitis
• Bowel obstruction/intussusception
• Poisoning (iron, insecticides, etc)

Dizziness/Syncope

Possible causes of dizziness and/or syncope in the pediatric population include:

• Dysrhythmias
• Aortic stenosis
• Hypovolemia (dehydration or blood loss)
• Seizures
• Hypoglycemia
• Intracranial lesion, with/without history of trauma
• Inner ear infection

Fever

In taking a history from a caregiver, ask specifically:

• Fever subjective or measured (if measured, what route used)
• Treatment attempted:
  1. Antipyretics (type, time of last dose, amount given; reasonable dose of acetaminophen is 10 to 15 mg/kg; children are often underdosed)
  2. Sponge bathing
  3. Cool dressing

Management of fever in children may vary among physicians and institutions. In the triage area, the following guidelines are useful in determining which patients' fevers warrant immediate attention:

- Fever in a newborn (younger than 12 weeks)
- Fever greater than 38.5° C measured rectally in a child older than 12 weeks but younger than 6 months
- Fever greater than 39.0° C measured rectally in a child older than 6 months
- Fever accompanied by any of the signs/symptoms included in the signs/symptoms list above

Headache

The following findings, when associated with headache, are warning signs that suggest serious pathology:

- Unusual severity
- Concomitant vomiting
- Concomitant ataxia
- Concomitant diplopia
- Lateralization of pain to one side
- Exacerbation by recumbent positioning
- Meningeal signs
- Toxic appearance
- Altered mental status, including irritability
- Seizures associated with pain
- Focal findings upon neurologic examination

Fever may produce headache in relatively benign conditions. Nevertheless, fever with headache, or vice versa, should raise the index of suspicion for serious illness.

Hematuria

The possible causes of hematuria in children are not quickly identified, but all the possible causes are potentially serious. Hematuria in a child warrants expedited care.

Joint Pain/Arthritis

The primary goal of the triage nurse in a presentation of arthritis, with or without associated limp, is to consider the following "red herrings" and to intervene appropriately:

- Ensure that there has not been trauma to the area, perhaps involving occult trauma to some other area, such as the head
- When the arthritic condition presents as a limp, ensure that the child is not ataxic; if ataxia is suspected, see "Limp" below

Apparent joint pain of the elbow and refusal to use an upper extremity in a toddler may represent nursemaid's elbow.

Limp

Acute onset of limp in children should be considered significant. Take care to ensure that the limp that the child's caretaker has observed is not ataxia. Consider the possibility of the following conditions in a child with a true limp:

- Septic arthritis
- Osteomyelitis
- Fracture
- Central nervous system abnormality

Mental Status Changes

Assessment of an irritable and/or lethargic child can be difficult, because irritability can be produced by fear and because lethargy can be produced by need for a good night's sleep. In evaluating children who are irritable or lethargic, look for clues that the cause may be related to one of the following:

- Infectious (sepsis, meningitis, pneumonia, arthritis, osteomyelitis, encephalitis, Reye's syndrome)
- Traumatic (head trauma, occult fracture, poisoning, abuse, lead poisoning)
- Metabolic (hypernatremia, hypoglycemia, hypocalcemia, uremia, acidosis, post seizure state)
- Other (paroxysmal atrial tachycardia, testicular/ovarian torsion, entrapment of viscus organ through a hernia, intussusception)

Painful Testes/Scrotum

Painful testes and/or scrotum should be evaluated immediately by a physician to rule out torsion of a testicle or incarcerated inguinal hernia. If a urine specimen can be easily obtained or a urine bag applied to an infant without undue stress, this may be done in the triage area.

Poisoning

Suspect poisoning if the symptoms "don't add up," especially if the child is a toddler, and may have gotten hold of a poisonous or toxic substance without the caregiver's knowledge. Ataxia, suggestive of systemic etiology, may masquerade as inability to use the lower extremities or a limp.

Do not induce vomiting if there has been ingestion of:

- Hydrocarbon
- Corrosive agent
- Strychnine

- Central nervous system depressant that has produced lethargy and/or respiratory depression

Rash, Petechiae, Purpura

Although triageurs often develop sophisticated skills in identifying rashes in children, the primary concerns of the triage nurse in evaluating a rash are as follows:

- Does it represent a contagious condition (when in doubt, isolate)
- Do the concomitant symptoms put the child at risk (eg, is there high fever, evidence of dehydration, sepsis)

Petechiae and/or purpura should be considered serious findings. A number of contagious and noncontagious, but serious, illnesses produce petechiae and purpura. A child with either should be evaluated by a physician immediately. Quick, but careful, evaluation of hemodynamic status is warranted. Note that meningococcemia and *Hemophilus influenzae* septicemia may produce petechiae or purpura. The child with a toxic appearance, fever, and/or meningeal signs should be considered emergently ill; meningococcemia and *H influenzae* infections may produce fulminant shock rapidly.[1,2]

Rashes in children are not uncommon. Standard pediatric textbooks and dermatology books include illustrations to guide the practitioner. A brief set of guidelines covering some of the commonly encountered childhood rashes is given below:

- *Measles (rubeola):* Erythematous maculopapular rash starts on face and gradually spreads downward. More severe on earlier sites of eruption and less severe on later sites. In later stages, takes on brownish appearance, and desquamation occurs. Accompanied by fever, conjunctivitis, Koplik's spots, general malaise, generalized lymphadenopathy.

- *Chickenpox:* Highly pruritic. Starts as macule, progresses to papule and then to vesicle. Distribution is centripedal, spreads to face and extremities; sparse on distal limbs. Accompanied by fever, lymphadenopathy.

- *Scarlet fever:* "Sandpaper" texture with erythema of skin; rash is more intense in folds of joints. Accompanied by sore throat, high fever, tachycardia greater than expected with fever. Tongue may be coated, red, swollen.

- *Impetigo*: Usually well localized, may itch. Has appearance of cellulitis with broken areas secondary to scratching. Patient is usually not febrile unless infection has spread.

- *Roseola:* Discrete rose-colored macule or maculopapules. Appear first on trunk, then spread to neck, face, and extremities. Does not itch. Fades with pressure. Accompanied by injected pharynx, cervical lymphadenopathy.

- *Drug reactions* (Stevens-Johnson syndrome, Kawasaki disease): Generalized presentation, may produce urticaria, pruritis, purpura, petechiae. Suspect this if child has been exposed to new drugs or other substances, either orally or topically, and has not had prodromal symptoms or contact with contagious disease.

Respiratory Distress/Drooling

Dyspnea

Severe dyspnea may be best judged by the observation of retracting, use of accessory muscles, grunting, flaring, and mental status changes. Potential causes of an increased respiratory rate and/or dyspnea may be broadly categorized as follows:

- *Upper airway*: Epiglottitis, croup, foreign body aspiration, asthma, bronchiolitis, trauma with swelling/edema, abscess (peritonsillar, retropharyngeal)
- *Lower airway/lungs*: Pneumonitis, pneumothorax

- *Cardiac*: Congestive heart failure
- *Metabolic*: Diabetic ketoacidosis, salicylate ingestion, sepsis

Respiratory Distress

- *Foreign body aspiration:* A frequent cause of respiratory distress in children, especially in the toddler. If the aspiration is recent, the child will probably be afebrile. The onset is generally sudden and often occurs while the child is eating or playing with small objects. The onset of symptoms may coincide with a momentary lack of supervision of the child. The symptoms are usually not progressive, although traumatic swelling or change in the object's position may worsen the dyspnea. Look for stridor and/or localized wheezing and marked accessory muscle effort.

- *Asthma/reactive airway disease*: Avoid attributing respiratory distress to asthma unless the child has a diagnosed history of asthma. If a child presents with wheezing for the first time, assume that an acute and emergent condition exists. Expiratory wheezing is commonly heard, but as an asthma exacerbation progresses wheezing may occur on inspiration as well. Wheezing will be generalized rather than localized. The absence of adventitious sounds may represent a loss of air exchange and impending respiratory failure. If an asthma exacerbation is brought on by an upper airway infection, the child may be febrile.

- *Infectious process*: The onset and course of symptoms are usually progressive, but symptoms may progress rapidly. In addition to respiratory distress, the child may be febrile and appear to be in a toxic condition.

  1. *Upper airway:* Infections can occur in the upper airway or in the pulmonary tissues. Stridor and drooling suggest upper airway infection and obstruction and may be produced by epiglottitis, laryngotracheobronchitis (croup), peritonsillar abscess, and retropharyngeal abscess. Handle the child minimally, reassure him or her as much as possible, and have a physician see the patient immediately. Keep

excitement and agitation to a minimum. Vital signs may be deferred if the nurse's approach frightens the child. If the temperature must be measured, use the axillary route. No attempt should be made to visualize or manipulate the airway by anyone other than personnel with expertise in intubation of children with upper airway obstruction.

2. *Pulmonary infection/pneumonia:* Pneumonia can seriously compromise a child's respiratory status. Breath sounds will be decreased in the affected area, and wheezing may be heard in the infected locale.

- *Allergic reaction*: Acute allergic reaction may rapidly precipitate respiratory distress. Usually symptoms are acute, perhaps arising after an insect bite or ingestion of unfamiliar food. Anaphylactic shock and respiratory failure can rapidly follow. Look for urticaria, erythema, periorbital swelling, and pruritus. Wheezing may be present, but breath sounds will fade as air exchange decreases.

- *Miscellaneous etiologies*:

  1. *Inhalation pneumonitis*: Associated with exposure to toxic fumes or smoke
  2. *Cardiac asthma*: Respiratory failure and adventitious sounds due to pulmonary congestion secondary to heart failure; examine patient for signs of congestive heart failure.

A history of cyanosis or apnea is an indication for urgent evaluation, even if the child appears well upon arrival at the hospital. Many hospitals will admit children with this history, regardless of physical findings, to rule out a missed sudden infant death syndrome diagnosis or a seizure disorder with apnea.

Seizure/Ataxia

Either of these presenting complaints should alert the triageur to institute immediate intervention. Ventilation and/or circulation may be put at risk by neurologic sequelae, so that a child with an altered mental status should be quickly but carefully evaluated for cardiopulmonary compromise. A physician should see the child immediately. Anticipate some or all of the following physician orders:

- Airway, oxygen with ventilation as needed
- Cardiac and hemodynamic status monitoring
- Dextrostick reading (obtain immediately)
- Labs: Standard electrolytes with calcium, magnesium, BUN, and glucose; CBC with platelets; sickle cell prep or other test if indicated; SGOT, PT, and PTT; blood and/or urine for toxicology screening; arterial blood gas measurements
- Intravenous line access

Shock

In children, shock may manifest itself in the early stages with cold mottled extremities, rapid pulses, and altered mental status. The blood pressure may not be alarmingly low in early shock because peripheral vasoconstriction may maintain the blood pressure despite low output. Nevertheless, the pulse pressure will often be decreased. Practitioners are reminded to unwrap swaddled infants to evaluate the hemodynamic status.

Generally, shock is not due to primary cardiac problems but is usually secondary to respiratory failure or loss of volume. Loss of volume may result from blood or fluid loss, or it may be relative, secondary to vascular dilation, as in sepsis.

Trauma

Trauma evaluation and management for adults and children are similar. Normal parameters for blood pressure in children are given in Table 11-2.

The relatively large size of the head and torso in children, coupled with their immature skeletal system, make these structures highly vulnerable to trauma.

Table 11-2 Blood Pressure Values in Children (Approximate Values, on Average)

Age	Systolic (mm Hg)	Diastolic (mm Hg)
Newborn	80	46
6–12 months	90	60
1–4 years	100	65
4–6 years	96	60
6–10 years	102	57
10–14 years	115	59

Source: Data from *Pediatrics* (1975; 56:3), American Academy of Pediatrics.

Traumatic injuries must be investigated to rule out abuse as the cause. The following findings *may* suggest abuse as the etiology:

- History of previous injuries
- History of premature birth or complicated neonatal period
- Conflicting histories:
  1. Between child and accompanying adult
  2. Between two or more adults accompanying child
- History that does not explain the physical findings
- Poor parent-child interaction
- Poor social situation
- Failure to thrive as determined by comparison of growth and development to standardized values

Torticollis

Torticollis often has a benign etiology, but consider and investigate these serious potential conditions:

- Phenothiazine ingestion

- Cervical spine trauma
- Intracranial lesion, especially at the posterior fossa

Vomiting

A relatively common presenting complaint among pediatric patients in the emergency department, vomiting can be associated with a number of serious illnesses. Vomiting associated with the following should warrant expedited, if not immediate, physician evaluation:

- Emesis containing bright red blood, "coffee ground material," or bilious material
- Vomiting that is preceded by abdominal pain (per history)
- Presence of abdominal pain between vomiting episodes
- Abdominal tenderness or guarding
- Signs of toxicity, including lethargy, irritability, weakness, altered mental status, tachycardia, tachypnea
- Central nervous system findings (headache, ataxia, nystagmus, neurologic examination with asymmetric findings)
- Evidence of dehydration
- Any vomiting that does not fit the picture of classic gastroenteritis (concomitant diarrhea, fever, associated illness in housemates)

Vomiting Blood and/or Blood in Stool

Gastrointestinal bleeding in children must be considered an emergency until proven otherwise. In young infants, intussusception may be associated with colicky symptoms and/or extreme lethargy.

Take a careful history in evaluating a child with apparent gastrointestinal bleeding. Red-colored foods such as beets, red-colored drinks, and the like can produce red-colored stools or emesis.

REFERENCES

1. Cosgriff JH, Anderson AL. *The Practice of Emergency Care.* Philadelphia: Lippincott; 1984:480-483.

2. Wintrobe J. *Harrison's Principles of Internal Medicine.* New York: McGraw-Hill; 1982:786,815,1804.

Appendix A

Acid-Base Disturbances

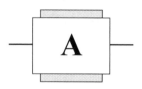

A

ACID-BASE DISTURBANCES

If the patient is in metabolic acidosis, he or she is said to have a *base deficit*. If the patient is in metabolic alkalosis, he or she is said to have a *base excess*. (A base excess may have the effect of correcting a respiratory acidosis, thus bringing the patient's total pH back toward normal. In such cases, even though the patient's pH may be normal, it is still called a base *excess* because it is *not a deficit* and because more bicarbonate is being retained by the kidneys than is normal.)

In the event of a base deficit requiring bicarbonate replacement, the amount of bicarbonate needed to correct the deficit may be calculated as follows:

$$\frac{\text{Base deficit x 4}}{\text{Patient's weight (in kg)}} = \text{Correct dose of bicarbonate (in mEq, delivered as sodium bicarbonate)}$$

CAUSATIVE RELATIONSHIPS WITHIN ACID-BASE DISTURBANCES

Acid-base disturbances have myriad causes. In evaluating possible causes, consider that either acidosis or alkalosis may be produced by a gain or loss of ions. The more commonly encountered possible causes of acid-base disturbance are given in Table A-1.

Table A-1 Hydrogen and Bicarbonate Relationship to pH

Problem	Hydrogen Ions	Bicarbonate Ions
Acidosis	Gain*	Loss‡
Alkalosis	Loss†	Gain§

* Acidosis related to a relative gain of hydrogen ions is often produced by the production of byproducts of anaerobic metabolism.

† Alkalosis secondary to a loss of hydrogen ions may occur with intractable vomiting or overzealous nasogastric suctioning without careful replacement of fluids and electrolytes.

‡ Acidosis can also result from loss of bicarbonate ions. These ions are lost through renal excretion or via the gastrointestinal tract. Acidosis due to a relative loss of bicarbonate is a serious side effect of severe diarrhea.

§ Alkalosis secondary to use of certain medications (check to see whether patient is using Aldomet) can be chronic in nature. During resuscitation, alkalosis may be produced by overdose of sodium bicarbonate.

Source: Adapted from *A Pocket Manual of Differential Diagnosis,* ed 2, (p 1–20) by SN Adler et al. with permission of Little, Brown and Company, © 1988.

ABBREVIATED LIST OF SOME POSSIBLE CAUSES OF ACID-BASE ABNORMALITIES

Respiratory Acidosis

- Ingestion or overdose of substances that depress respiratory function
- Central nervous system injury or infarct
- Neuromuscular disease
- Myopathies affecting respiratory muscles
- Diaphragmatic paralysis
- Airway obstruction
- Respiratory insufficiency
- Cardiac insufficiency
- Restrictive lung disease
- Pulmonary embolism

- Pneumothorax, hemothorax
- Trauma to chest
- Smoke inhalation
- Severe scoliosis
- Improper artificial ventilation

Respiratory Alkalosis

- Voluntary hyperventilation
- Anxiety
- Pain
- Hypoxia
- Fever
- Head trauma
- Intracranial lesion
- Salicylate toxicity
- Central nervous system infection (eg, meningitis)
- Cerebrovascular accident
- Congestive heart failure producing tachypnea
- Pneumonia producing tachypnea
- Pulmonary embolism producing tachypnea
- Adult respiratory distress syndrome
- High altitudes
- Sepsis
- Drugs
  1. Xanthine
  2. Catecholamine
  3. Nicotine
- Heat exposure

Metabolic Acidosis

- Renal failure
- Ketoacidosis
- Lactic acidosis

- Toxins:
  1. Aspirin
  2. Methanol
  3. Ethylene glycol
  4. Toluene
  5. Paraldehyde
- Hyperosmolar nonketotic coma
- Gastrointestinal loss
  1. Diarrhea
  2. Loss of small bowel function (status post surgical resection)
- Renal loss:
  1. Malfunction of renal tubules
  2. Carbonic anhydrase inhibitor use
- Rapid fluid resuscitation without administration of bicarbonate
- Administration or ingestion of acidifying substances
- Sulfur ingestion

Metabolic Alkalosis

- Vomiting
- Nasogastric suctioning
- Drainage from gastrointestinal fistula or via gastrointestinal tract
- Diuretic use
- Cystic fibrosis
- Aldosteronism
- Potassium depletion
- Administration or ingestion of alkalinizing agents
  1. Citrate
  2. Lactate
  3. Antacids
  4. Massive blood or plasma transfusion
  5. Large doses of anionic antibiotics (eg, penicillin)
  6. Hypercalcemia not due to parathyroid abnormalities (eg, multiple myeloma, bone tumors)

Appendix B

Evaluation Tips and Techniques

EVALUATION OF THE ABDOMEN

Subjective

- *Careful history of onset:* What was the time of onset (ask patient to be as specific as possible)? Was the onset sudden or gradual? What were the first symptoms experienced? What is the character of the pain (burning, stabbing, etc)? Has the pain moved? Does it radiate (ie, does it go anywhere)? Has the pain worsened? (Using a scale from 1 to 10 may help the patient quantitate his or her pain and any changes in intensity he may have experienced) Does the pain increase on inspiration?

- *Age of patient:* Appendicitis seldom occurs in infancy; it is most common in adolescents. Obstruction of the large intestine by cancerous stricture is seldom seen before 30 years of age and infrequently before 40, but it is the most common cause of obstruction in persons older than 40 years of age. Acute pancreatitis is seldom seen in young adults, except if there is a long history of alcohol abuse.[1]

- *Nausea and vomiting:* Are they concomitant? Did they occur before, during, or sometime after the onset of pain? If vomiting, how many times? What has been the character of the emesis?

- *Bowel activity:* Usually regular? (Define regularity with the patient.) When was the last bowel movement? What was the character? Diarrhea? Blood in stool? Increased pain with bowel movement?

- *Detailed menstrual history*: Exact date of last period. Did the period differ from "usual" (heavier or lighter flow, more pain than usual)? Ask about history of intercourse (pain with intercourse, unprotected intercourse).

- *History of serous illnesses:* Ask specifically about jaundice, melena, hematemesis, hematuria, weight loss.

- *History of concomitant fever*: Document recent use of antipyretics (within previous 24 hours).

- *Trauma and/or intoxication*: Question patient about any trauma he or she may have sustained and about ingestion of noxious or toxic substances, including alcohol.

Objective

- General posture and degree of comfort of patient
- Observe posture, especially when patient is asked to lie flat (must the knees be drawn to the chest?)
- Take vital signs carefully, looking especially for signs of hemodynamic compromise; pain may increase the pulse rate, blood pressure, and respirations; always take orthostatic vital signs
- Measure and document temperature
- Observe abdomen for break in the skin, discoloration, ascites, generalized distension, localized swelling, presence of hernia
- Auscultate abdomen before attempting palpation; warm stethoscope before placing it on patient's abdomen

- Listen in quiet area for a full 60 seconds in each quadrant using systematic pattern of auscultation; document all sounds heard, if any; listen carefully for presence of bruit

- Palpate abdomen with warm hands, again using systematic approach to all quadrants; start with area farthest from site of the pain, if it is localized, and work your way toward it; document patient's report of pain as you palpate; feel for rigidity and/or masses; assess for rebound tenderness (this part of the examination may be minimized if patient will be seen quickly by physician)

- Obtain urine, stool, and/or emesis samples, if possible, and guaiac the samples

REFERENCE

1. Cope Z. *The Early Diagnosis of the Acute Abdomen*. London: Oxford University Press; 1972:48-78.

EVALUATION OF EXTREMITIES

In assessing an extremity, evaluation of the following helps minimize the chance of missing a serious finding:

- Carriage and positioning of extremity as patient presents

- Presence of any obvious deformity, to include all joints and all bones suspended between joints (splint per protocol as needed)

- Color and condition of skin

- Neurovascular status (sensory and motor examination, presence of pulses in comparison to contralateral extremity, if normal)

- Capillary refill time (quantitate)

- Measurement of range of motion (if no obvious deformity present and severe pain does not result), both passive and active; include range of motion of fingers or toes

- Skin temperature in comparison to other areas of the body, especially contralateral extremity
- Evaluate sensory function using standard dermatome map to identify sensory deficits
- Compare affected extremity to contralateral extremity and document:
    1. Obvious deformity
    2. Tenderness
    3. Skin temperature
    4. Capillary refill time
    5. Swelling
    6. Discoloration, including erythema, ecchymosis
    7. Breaks in skin
    8. Edema (pitting or nonpitting)
- Observation and palpation to include specific examination of:
    1. Fingers:
        —Metacarpal/phalangeal tenderness
        —Integrity of collateral ligaments
        —Range of motion
        —Flexion and extension of digits
        —Optional: two-point discrimination
    2. Hand:
        —Metacarpal/phalangeal tenderness
    3. Wrist:
        —Metacarpal/phalangeal tenderness
        —Navicular tenderness
    4. Forearm:
        —Pronation and supination
    5. Elbow:
        —Pronation and supination
        —Examine wrist and shoulder, forearm and humerus
        —Range of motion
    6. Toes:
        —Metatarsals
        —Capillary refill; skin temperature, color

   7. Foot:

   —Metatarsal/phalangeal tenderness

   —Palpate at base of fifth metatarsal

   —Palpate pedal pulses: posterior tibial and dorsalis
     pedis

   8. Ankle

   9. Lower leg

- Elicit Homans' sign (document presence or absence)

EVALUATION OF THE EYE

- Compare appearance of eyes to each other

- *Visual acuity*: Using standardized Snellen's chart at 20
  ft, document acuity in both eyes. Uncorrected vision
  (without glasses) may be compared to corrected vision.

- *Evaluation of external ocular movements (EOMs)*:
  EOM functional assessment provides information
  about the function of the fourth and sixth cranial nerves
  and the muscles they innervate. Their function can be
  affected by trauma and some infectious processes. To
  conduct the EOM examination follow these steps:

   1. Evaluate patient's ability to cooperate. If coopera-
      tive:

   2. Have patient gaze straight ahead, and match his or
      her gaze with your own.

   3. Instruct patient to hold head steady and to follow
      your moving finger with his or her eyes as you
      move it to the left, right, up, and down. If patient is
      able to look in all planes, EOMs are intact.

   4. Observe and document presence of nystagmus, par-
      ticularly in patients who have seizure disorders and
      are taking anticonvulsant medication.

- *Pupil response*:

   1. Size (in millimeters)

   2. Equality of size

   3. Shape

   4. Reaction to light

5. Accommodation

- *Checklist of findings*:
  1. Redness
  2. Periorbital swelling
  3. Tearing
  4. Foreign body
  5. Clarity of anterior chamber

EVALUATION OF HEMODYNAMIC STATUS

- Observation of skin color, temperature, condition
- Evaluation of level of consciousness
- Evaluation of strength of all peripheral pulses, to include quantitated comparison of strength
- Assessment of jugular vein appearance
- Assessment for postural hypotension (orthostatic hypotension): Drop of 20 mm Hg in systolic blood pressure or 10 mm Hg in diastolic pressure between supine and standing readings; a smaller drop may be considered significant if the patient is symptomatic (ie, displays dizziness)[1]
- Auscultation of heart sounds to document presence or absence of extra sounds, murmurs, rubs, etc
- Auscultation of breath sounds to document presence or absence of adventitious sounds, particularly rales
- Careful evaluation of pulse quality and regularity: A patient whose arterial pulse is not regular, and whose pulse irregularity is not due to fluctuations in the inspiratory/expiratory cycle (sinus arrhythmia), should have electrocardiographic evaluation; the following list of cardiac rhythms describes the more commonly encountered dysrhythmias that may produce an irregular arterial pulse:
  1. Atrial fibrillation
  2. Sinus block, pause, or arrest
  3. Atrial flutter with variable conduction
  4. Second-degree heart block type I

5. Second-degree heart block type II with variable conduction
6. Third-degree heart block with unreliable ventricular escape pacemaker
7. Shifting heart block
8. Frequently occurring ectopy/extrasystole

REFERENCE

1. Tideiksaar R, Kay A. What causes falls: a logical diagnostic approach. *Geriatrics*. 1986;41:32-51.

NEUROLOGIC EVALUATION

- Orientation to person, place, time, and events
- Ease of arousability
- Glasgow coma scale:

  1. Eye opening (assesses arousability): Evaluate for spontaneous eye opening to speech or painful stimuli. Speak in clear, adequately loud voice. Touch patient to help establish contact. To elicit painful stimulus response, apply pressure to fingernail beds.

Spontaneous eye opening	4
Opens eyes to speech	3
Opens eyes to pain	2
No eye opening	1
Eyes closed from swelling	1

  2. Verbal response: Make contact with patient; get his or her attention and then attempt conversation. Provide "wait time" to allow for slow or delayed response.

Oriented to person, place, time	5
Talks but is confused about person, place, time	4
Uses random words, makes no sense	3
Moaning or groaning but no words	2
No verbal response	1

3. Motor response: Give simple commands, allow time to respond. Record best response. Provide painful stimulus if patient does not respond to commands. Avoid interpreting reflexive movements such as grasp or posturing as a response.

Obeys commands	6
Localizes pain	5
Flexion withdrawal	4
Abnormal flexion at elbow with internal rotation of wrist	3
Abnormal extension of the arm at the elbow and internal rotation of shoulder	2
No response	1

- Limb movement:

   1. Arms: Instruct patient to move arm laterally, to lift arm against gravity, and to move arm against resistance. If left and right have different responses, record separately. To evaluate for drift, have patient hold arms out with palms turned up and close eyes. Observe for 10 to 15 seconds for downward drift:

      —Normal power: Moves as instructed

      —Mild weakness: Moves with difficulty against resistance and gravity

—Severe weakness: Great difficulty against gravity, cannot move against resistance

—Spastic flexion: Flexes arm only

—Extension: Extends elbow and externally rotates wrist

—No response: No effort made

—Drift: One arm drifts downward

2. Legs: Instruct patient to move leg laterally and to lift leg against gravity and against resistance. Document differences in right and left response:

—Normal power: Moves as instructed

—Mild weakness: Moves legs with difficulty against resistance and gravity

—Severe weakness: Great difficulty against gravity, cannot move against resistance

—Extension: Extends leg

—No response: no effort made

- Eye signs:

1. Pupils: Document size, reaction to light (darken room; hold eyelid open while closing opposite eye; move small, bright light toward patient from side; shine directly into eye; record reaction of each pupil):

—Size (in millimeters)

—Equality of size

—Shape

—Reaction to light

—Accommodation

2. Extraocular movements:

Evaluation of EOMs is an important part of the neurologic examination. EOM functional assessment provides information about the function of the fourth and sixth cranial nerves. Their function can be affected by trauma and some infectious processes. To conduct the EOM examination, follow these steps:

—Evaluate patient's ability to cooperate. If cooperative:

—Have patient gaze straight ahead and match his or her gaze with your own.

—Instruct patient to hold head steady and to follow your moving finger with his or her eyes as you move it to the left, right, up, and down. If patient is able to look in all planes, EOMs are intact.

—Observe and document presence of nystagmus, particularly in patients who have seizure disorders and are taking anticonvulsant medication.

• Cardiovascular signs:

Assess carefully for cardiovascular stability. See Table B-1 for common cardiovascular problems that are associated with neurologic trauma.

Table B-1 Cardiovascular Problems Associated With Neurotrauma

Problem	Etiology	Clinical Features
Spinal shock	Loss of sympathetic reflex tone in spinal cord injury (SCI)	Onset in immediate posttraumatic phase. Hypotension and bradycardia
Autonomic dysreflexia	Return of sympathetic tone after spinal shock has subsided in SCI; massive unchecked sympathetic stimulation of tissues	Onset after spinal shock phase has subsided; bradycardia, hypertension, headache, reddened face, diaphoresis above level of lesion
Cushing's syndrome (triad)	Increased intracranial pressure (head injury)	Associated with increased intracranial pressure, whether sudden or progressing. Bradycardia, systolic hypertension, widened pulse pressure

EVALUATION OF PAIN

Subjective

- Onset, duration, location, concomitant symptoms
- Does it keep patient awake or awaken patient from sleep?
- Does anything relieve it?
- Note words used to describe character (eg, "sticking me with a knife," "crushing me," "burning," etc) and document these words in quotation marks.
- Use a scale from 1 to 10, with 1 at the lowest and 10 as the worst pain ever experienced. Ask patient to choose a number on the scale. This can be helpful in assessing any subsequent changes in the intensity of the pain the patient experiences, and documentation in the triage area will provide baseline information. Children can be shown a graphic picture of a number line and asked to pick a spot on the picture.

Objective

- Guarded positioning
- Tensing of voluntary muscles
- Facial grimacing
- Increased pulse, blood pressure, and/or respirations
- Evidence of inflammation at site
- Rubbing, cradling, or pulling body part
- Tense body posture
- Apparent fatigue

EVALUATION OF RESPIRATORY STATUS

Careful evaluation of the patient's respiratory status can determine whether the patient is critically ill, seriously ill, or one of the walking wounded. A quick assessment of respiratory status includes the following:

- Evaluation of patient's comfort, the effort that he or she is putting into breathing (use of accessory muscles, nasal flaring), mental status, ability to speak in complete sentences

- Examination of peripheral vasculature for cyanosis (nail beds, conjunctivae)

- Evaluation of respiratory rate and ratio of inspiratory to expiratory volume (normal ratio in adults is 1:2)

- Auscultation of breath sounds in systematic manner to include upper airway (over trachea), bronchial sounds, vesicular sounds; adventitious sounds should be evaluated before and after patient is asked to cough

- Evaluation of heart rate with respect to respiratory distress

- Evaluation of patient's ability to lie flat or with head of bed only moderately elevated

- Evaluation of blood pressure, particularly eliciting pulsus paradoxus

A more thorough assessment of respiratory status should include evaluation of the following:

- Patient's ability to speak comfortably, his or her ability to answer questions with full sentences rather than short, labored responses (history may best be provided by bystanders or caregivers)

- Appearance:
  1. Skin color, especially around lips, nail beds, conjunctivae
  2. Respiratory rate, presence of tachypnea or bradypnea
  3. Chest wall movement, symmetry and depth of expansion
  4. Presence of diaphoresis
  5. If sequelae are long term, assess for dehydration
  6. Skin temperature (assess peripheral and central structures)
  7. Psychologic status (presence of anxiety, agitation, sense of impending doom)
  8. Use of accessory breathing muscles

- Audibility of breathing (assess without stethoscope)
  1. Audible wheezing
  2. Audible stridor
  3. Snoring sounds
- Assessment of cough (dry, productive, "wet")
- Rate, quality, depth of respirations (assess for full 60 seconds)
- Auscultation of breath sounds
  1. Type of sound (normal or adventitious)
  2. Presence of rales (do not clear with cough)
  3. Presence of rhonchi (may improve or clear with cough; rales and rhonchi may be charted as "crackles")
  4. Presence of pleural friction rub
  5. Presence of decreased or distant sounds (when comparing sounds heard in various areas of chest)
  6. Absence of sounds (usually indicates urgent situation)
  7. Relative equality of sounds heard during systematic auscultation
- Palpation of chest:
  1. Bilateral, abnormal chest wall movement
  2. Presence of crepitus
  3. Presence of pain elicited by palpation
- Patient posture and carriage:
  1. Upright
  2. Barrel chested
  3. Unable to lie flat or with head of bed below $45°$
- Specific vital sign changes:
  1. Dyspnea and shortness of breath usually produce tachycardia
  2. Tachypnea is an early sign of respiratory distress and hypoxia
  3. Bradypnea may suggest sequelae involving neurologic system (bradypnea is usually a late sign of hypoxia; Kussmaul's pattern is associated with diabetic ketoacidosis; Cheyne-Stokes pattern associated with neurologic sequelae)

- Blood pressure assessment (presence of pulsus paradoxus)
- Temperature assessment (oral readings may be decreased by mouth breathing)

HELPFUL REMINDERS IN EVALUATING OXYGENATION AND VENTILATION STATUS

Ventilation and oxygenation, although directly related, are not the same thing. Adequate oxygenation does not guarantee adequate ventilation, and vice versa. Use of continuous oxygen saturation monitors does not provide direct information about ventilatory status. See Table B-2 for arterial blood gas values within normal limits.

Carbon dioxide must be measured against the patient's respiratory rate. A tachypneic patient should have a lowered carbon dioxide level. For example, an asthmatic patient with a respiratory rate of 32 per minute should have a relatively low carbon dioxide level. If the carbon dioxide tension is measured at 40 mm Hg, this patient may be retaining carbon dioxide in relative terms.

Table B-2 Normal Arterial Blood Gas Values

Parameter	Normal Value
Oxygen tension	80 to 100 mm Hg (in patient without chronic obstructive pulmonary disease)
Carbon dioxide tension	35 to 45 mm Hg
pH	7.35 to 7.45
Bicarbonate	22 to 26 mEq/L
Oxygen saturation	≥95%
Base excess	0 ± 2 mEq/L

Appendix C

Cardiac Arrhythmias

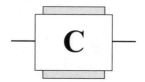

CARDIAC ARRHYTHMIAS

Criteria for rates are based on the expected rates for adult hearts.

NORMAL SINUS RHYTHM

- Regular discharge of the sinus node producing consistent P wave activity (P waves are upright in leads I, II, and aVF) with a constant PR interval.
- Rate in the adult patient is 60 to 100 beat/min.
- Rhythm is regular or essentially regular.
- Observe for ischemic changes (ST segment distortion, T wave inversion), particularly in leads V_2 and V_5.

BRADYCARDIA

- Associated with:
  1. Parasympathetic discharge or event (vasovagal episode)
  2. Ischemia
  3. Infarct
  4. Drug toxicity (especially β-blocker and digitalis toxicity)

5. Increased intracranial pressure
6. Carotid sinus pressure
7. Paradoxic response to hypoxemia

- Cardiac output is at risk with all bradycardias, and will worsen when atrial activity is lost

Supraventricular Bradycardia

- May produce escape pacemaker activity
- Sinus node rate is less than 60 beat/min in an adult, sinus rhythm is regular
- Node rate is less than 40 beat/min in an adult, regular rhythm (this signals failure of the sinus node, AV node is working as an escape pacemaker)

Ventricular (Idioventricular) Bradycardia

- Slow escape rhythm in complete heart block or with loss of supraventricular activity
- Life-threatening rhythm

TACHYCARDIA

- Associated with:
    1. Sympathetic discharge or event
    2. Valvular dysfunction (especially of the mitral and aortic valves)
    3. Preexcitation syndromes (such as Wolff-Parkinson-White syndrome)
    4. Paradoxic events
    5. Drug toxicity (stimulants and adrenergics)
    6. Reflexive response to decreased tissue perfusion
    7. Fever
    8. Pain
    9. Anxiety
    10. Congestive heart failure (if the patient is not on β blockers)
    11. Thyrotoxicosis

Supraventricular

- Sinus tachycardia
    1. Rate is 100 to 140 beat/min
    2. P waves present or "buried"
    3. Narrow QRS complex
- Atrial tachycardia
    1. Rate at least 140 beat/min; classically it is greater than 160 beat/min
    2. P waves may be present but will have different morphology from sinus beats
- Paroxysmal atrial tachycardia
    1. Absolutely regular rhythm
    2. Rate greater than 140 to 150 beat/min
- Atrial fibrillation with rapid ventricular response
    1. Irregularly irregular rhythm
    2. Rhythm is said to have an uncontrolled ventricular response when rate is greater than 100 beat/min
- Atrial flutter with rapid ventricular response
    1. May be difficult to distinguish from other forms of supraventricular tachycardia
    2. Appearance of flutter waves in the baseline when rate is slowed will make the diagnosis
- Junctional or nodal tachycardia
    1. Absence of P waves or inverted P waves in lead II occurring before or after the QRS complex
    2. QRS morphology essentially normal
    3. May be difficult to distinguish from other forms of supraventricular tachycardia when rate is fast

Ventricular

- Ventricular tachycardia
    1. Essentially regular rhythm
    2. Rate greater than 100 beat/min
    3. No P waves or P wave activity dissociated with ventricular activity
    4. Widened QRS complex

- Although supraventricular tachycardia with aberrant conduction can masquerade as ventricular tachycardia, one should assume the worst of the two (ventricular), until the situation is proven otherwise.
    1. The patient's clinical status determines the severity of the emergency.

ECTOPIC BEATS

- Causes
    1. Irritability of foci
    2. Escape phenomenon (in conjunction with bradycardia)

Early

Supraventricular

- Premature atrial contractions
    1. Represent irritable electrical foci in the atria
    2. Characterized by early timing
    3. P wave will differ in morphology from P waves of sinus beats
    4. P wave is upright in lead II
    5. PR interval may vary from that in sinus beats
    6. Morphology of the QRS complex is normal
- Premature junctional or nodal contractions
    1. Represent irritable electrical foci in the junctional region or atrioventricular node
    2. Characterized by early timing
    3. P wave will differ in morphology from P waves in sinus beats
    4. P wave is inverted in lead II
    5. P waves may occur before, during, or after the QRS complex, which has normal morphology

Ventricular

- Premature ventricular contractions:

1. Represent ventricular irritability until proven other-wise
2. Widened QRS complex with bizarre morphology, often with polarity opposite that of normally con-ducted beats
3. If P wave is present, the PR interval will differ from that in normal conduction
4. Often accompanied by a fully compensatory pause
5. Large amount of voltage is often seen

Late

Suggest failure of a higher pacemaker, particularly the sinus node. These ectopic beats are also called escape beats.

- Nodal/junctional:
  1. No P wave or an inverted P wave in lead II before or after the QRS complex
  2. Essentially normal QRS morphology
- Ventricular:
  1. Widened QRS complex with bizarre morphology
  2. Often with polarity opposite that of normally con-ducted beats
  3. If P wave is present, the PR interval will differ from normal conduction
  4. Often accompanied by a fully compensatory pause
  5. Large amount of voltage is often seen

HEART BLOCKS AT THE ATRIO-VENTRICULAR NODE

- Causes:
  1. Aging
  2. Drug toxicity
  3. Ischemia
  4. Infarct
  5. Electrolyte imbalance

- First degree:
    1. PR interval greater than 0.20 second
    2. PR interval constant
    3. All P waves followed by QRS complex
- Second degree:
    1. Type I/Wenckebach's phenomenon
        —PR wave lengthens in cycles
        —One P wave is unconducted to ventricles per cycle
        —Ventricular rhythm is regularly irregular, producing groups of beats
        —RR interval shortens through cycle
    2. Type II
        —PR interval constant; may be prolonged (greater than 0.20 second)
        —P waves unconducted to ventricles
        —Ventricular rhythm may be regular or irregular, depending upon regularity of conduction
        —May produce long intervals of ventricular asystole if atrioventricular node fails to conduct sequences of impulses
- Third degree:
    1. Complete loss of conduction at site of the atrioventricular tissue
    2. PR internal completely variable; may appear to have relationship, but close examination will reveal no relationship
    3. P waves unconducted to ventricles
    4. Ventricular rhythm generally regular in early stages of rhythm onset; regularity may deteriorate as blood flow decreases
    5. Ventricular escape rhythm provides pulse; QRS complex will widen and change morphology as site of ventricular pacemaker moves lower in ventricular conduction system

A patient whose arterial pulse is not regular and whose pulse irregularity is not due to fluctuations in the inspiratory/expiratory cycle (sinus arrhythmia) should undergo electrocardiography. The following list of cardiac rhythms describes the more commonly encountered dysrhythmias that may produce an irregular arterial pulse:

- Aberrantly conducted beats
- Atrioventricular dissociation without ventricular escape pacemaker function
- Atrial fibrillation
- Sinus block, pause, or arrest
- Atrial flutter with variable conduction
- Second-degree heart block type I
- Second-degree heart block type II with variable conduction
- Third-degree heart block with unreliable ventricular escape pacemaker
- Shifting heart block
- Frequently occurring ectopy/extrasystole

BIBLIOGRAPHY

Marriott HJL. *Practical Electrocardiography*. 7th ed. Baltimore: Williams & Wilkins; 1983.

Appendix D

Diabetic Ketoacidosis and Hyperosmolar Nonketotic Coma

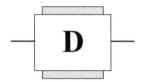

COMPARISON OF DIABETIC KETOACIDOSIS AND HYPEROSMOLAR NONKETOTIC COMA

Feature	Hyperosmolar Nonketotic Coma	Diabetic Ketoacidosis
Predisposing type of diabetes	Type II	Type I
Likelihood of underlying renal or vascular disease	85%	15%
Respiratory symptoms	None or Kussmaul's respirations	Hyperventilation/ Kussmaul's respirations
Breath odor	None	Fruity or acetone
Gastrointestinal symptoms	Rare	Abdominal pain, anorexia, nausea, vomiting, diarrhea
Neurological status	Depressed sensorium; may have focal seizures, nystagmus	Depressed sensorium

Feature	Hyperosmolar Nonketotic Coma	Diabetic Ketoacidosis
Fluid status	Very dehydrated	Moderately dehydrated
Acid-base balance	No acidosis	Acidosis
Serum glucose	Usually >800 mg/dL	<800 mg/dL
Serum ketones	Absent	Present
Urinary ketones	Absent or trace	Present
Potassium	Normal or high	May be low, normal, or high
Bicarbonate	>16 mEq/L	<10 mEq/L
pH	Normal	<7.25
Carbon dioxide	Normal	<10 mEq/L
Blood urea nitrogen	High	High
Anion gap	10 to 12 mEq/L	>12 mEq/L

Appendix E

Electrolyte Imbalances and Their Clinical Features

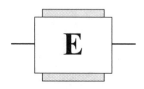

ELECTROLYTE IMBALANCES AND THEIR CLINICAL FEATURES

- Sodium
    1. Normal range, 135 to 145 mEq/L
    2. Hyponatremia:
    —Malaise
    —Nausea/vomiting
    —Headache
    —Confusion, lethargy
    —Convulsions, coma
    3. Hypernatremia:
    —Thirst
    —Oliguria
    —Confusion, lethargy
    —Muscle weakness, twitching
    —Convulsions, coma
- Potassium
    1. Normal range, 3.5 to 5.0 mEq/L
    2. Hypokalemia:
    —Intestinal colic, diarrhea
    —Muscle weakness ascending from the lower extremities *but spares respiratory muscles*

—Flaccid paralysis

—Cardiac dysrhythmia

—Flattened T waves, ST depression, U waves

3. Hyperkalemia:

—Decreased gastrointestinal function

—Flaccid paralysis

—Muscle weakness ascending from lower extremities (*includes respiratory muscles*)

—Increased urinary output

—Cardiac conduction abnormalities

—Peaked T waves, lengthened PR interval, widened QRS complex

- Chloride

  1. Normal range, 95 to 109 mEq/L (*Note: Chloride derangement has its most dangerous effect on serum sodium and potassium levels*)
  2. Hypochloremia: Clinical signs consistent with sodium and potassium derangement
  3. Hyperchloremia: Clinical signs consistent with sodium and potassium derangement

- Calcium

  1. Normal range, 8.5 to 10.5 mg/dL
  2. Hypocalcemia:

  —Muscle twitching, cramping

  —Positive Chvostek's and Trousseau's signs

  —Facial grimacing

  —Facial and digital paresthesia

  —Carpopedal spasms

  —Tetany

  3. Hypercalcemia:

  —Anorexia

  —Nausea/vomiting

  —Abdominal pain

  —Constipation

  —Headache

—Muscle weakness

—Generalized fatigue

- Phosphorus
  1. Normal range, 2.5 to 4.5 mg/dL
  2. Hypophosphoremia:

  —Vitamin D deficiency

  —Skeletal deformity (including rickets)

  —Soft bones

  —Poor dentition

  3. Hyperphosphoremia: Renal failure

- Magnesium
  1. Normal range, 1.5 to 2.5 mEq/L
  2. Hypomagnesemia:

  —Insomnia

  —Increased deep tendon reflexes

  —Positive Chvostek's and Trousseau's signs

  —Lower extremity cramping

  —Twitching, tremors

  —Confusion, central nervous system stimulation, convulsions

  —Cardiac dysrhythmias

  3. Hypermagnesemia:

  —Somnolence

  —Hypotension

  —Flushing, sweating

  —Central nervous system depression

  —Bradycardia, decreased cardiac excitability

  —Weak pulse

  —Weak deep tendon reflexes

  —Flaccid paralysis

  —Respiratory depression

Appendix F

Pathology Associated with Skin Color Changes

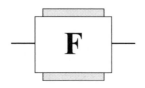

PATHOLOGY ASSOCIATED WITH SKIN COLOR CHANGES

- Flushing:
    1. Allergic reaction/anaphylaxis
    2. Carbon monoxide poisoning
    3. Heat exposure/hyperthermia
    4. Radiation exposure
    5. Angioneurotic edema

- Cyanosis:
    1. Hypoxemia
    2. Hypothermia
    3. Cyanide poisoning
    4. Ventilation/perfusion mismatch (shunting)

- Jaundice:
    1. Liver disease/hepatitis
    2. Ingestion of hepatic toxins
    3. Increased red blood cell break down
    4. Use of quinine

- Pallor:
    1. Poor tissue perfusion (hypotension, anemia, hypoxemia, sepsis)
    2. Hypothermia
    3. Frostbite

Appendix G

Reference List of Signs

REFERENCE LIST OF SIGNS

Battle's sign: Swelling and discoloration (ecchymosis) behind one or both ears associated with head trauma. Suggestive of a basilar skull fracture.

Chvostek's sign: Spasm of the muscles in the cheek and around the mouth in response to stimulus of cranial nerve VII. Suggestive of hypocalcemia and/or hypomagnesemia.

Cushing's triad: Decreased heart rate, increased systolic blood pressure, widened pulse pressure. Suggestive of increased intracranial pressure.

Grey Turner's sign: Subcutaneous bruising around the flanks. Suggestive of a retroperitoneal hematoma

Hamman's crunch: Crunching sound heard upon auscultation of the precordium, synchronous with the heartbeat. Produced by the heart's motion working against air that has collected in mediastinal tissues. Air-filled structures in proximity to the mediastinum have been interrupted, allowing air to leak into the mediastinum, producing mediastinal emphysema. May be caused by alveolar rupture, tracheal tear, bronchial tear, or esophageal tear. May be associated with pneumothorax, hemothorax, or respiratory failure.[1]

Homans' sign: Pain in calf elicited with dorsiflexion of ankle. Positive Homans' sign is associated with presence of thrombus and diminished blood flow to lower leg.

Pulse pressure: Difference between systolic pressure and diastolic pressure. Indicates the "reserve power" present in the circulation.

Raccoon eyes: Swelling and discoloration around both eyes associated with head trauma. Suggestive of a basilar skull fracture.

Trousseau's sign: Carpal-pedal spasm after occlusion of blood flow to the hand. Suggestive of hypocalcemia and/or hypomagnesemia.

REFERENCE

1. McGraw JP. Triage of a patient exhibiting Hamman's crunch after a fall. *J Emerg Nurs.* 1987; 13:1, 64–65.

Index